D1810159

FOOTBALL
On This Day

FOOTBALL
On This Day

*History, Facts & Figures
from Every Day of the Year*

JOE MEWIS & ROB BURNETT

FOOTBALL
On This Day

History, Facts & Figures from Every Day of the Year

All statistics, facts and figures are correct as of 1st September 2023

© Rob Burnett and Joe Mewis

Rob Burnett and Joe Mewis have asserted their rights in accordance with the Copyright, Designs and Patents Act 1988 to be identified as the authors of this work.

Pitch Publishing
9 Donnington Park,
85 Birdham Road,
Chichester,
West Sussex,
PO20 7AJ
www.pitchpublishing.co.uk
info@pitchpublishing.co.uk

First published 2008
Updated 2023

All rights reserved. No part of this publication may be reproduced, stored in a retrieval system, or transmitted in any form or by any means, electronic, mechanical, photocopying, recording or otherwise, without the prior permission in writing of the publisher and the copyright owners.

A catalogue record for this book is available from the British Library.

ISBN: 978 1 80150 893 3

Printed and bound in Great Britain by TJ Books, Padstow

ACKNOWLEDGEMENTS

Thanks to Paul and all those at Pitch for taking a chance on us, Tom and Annemarie for helping us get the project started by putting me up, Sue Gyford and Nuala McKay for encouragement and advice, Emily for her support and patience and most of all to Joe, for being a great co-author.

Rob Burnett – September 2008

Thanks to all at Pitch Publishing, Lenny Austin for helping set up www.onthisfootballday.com, where the idea for this book began and Gareth Christian-Lim for the cover design. Props to everyone who's supported the website and all our mates and colleagues who have chipped in with their favourite footy memories – you know who you are. Thanks also to Mum, Zoe, Pete and the family and finally to Rob for all the hard work over the last year.

Joe Mewis – September 2008

INTRODUCTION

Welcome to *Football: On This Day*. During the barren football-free months of summer 2007 we set up a website called www.onthisfootballday.com to explore those moments in football that might otherwise slip under the radar, and we have now selected our favourites for this book.

Other than the usual rousing title wins or derby-day victories, we've all got our favourite footballing memories, be it a moment of inspiration on the pitch, a 20-man brawl or whatever comedy antics Newcastle United are up to at any given moment.

In a climate where Sky Sports try and convince us that football began with the Premier League in 1992 we thought it was time to go through the ages, from 14th century kick-abouts to the mega-bucks all-encompassing football industry of today and bring you stories from every day of the year, inspired by endless pub debates.

As well as simply remembering the events that made us laugh, cry, or shake our heads in disbelief, we have spent months reading books and newspapers rooting out the best footballing tit-bits which provide a snapshot of the diverse and often bizarre world of football.

We have always tried to concentrate on the funny or unusual rather than simply results or statistics, and we hope reading the book will allow you to reminisce, laugh, and perhaps even learn something new.

Rob Burnett and Joe Mewis – September 2008

FOOTBALL
On This Day

JANUARY

JANUARY 1

When Sir Stanley Matthews signed for Blackpool in 1947 his new manager Joe Smith said: 'You're 32, do you think you can make it for another couple of years?' Sir Stan would go on to play at the top until he was 50, finally retiring in 1965 and it was on this day that year that he became the first footballer ever to receive a knighthood. Despite being the first winner of the Ballon d'Or, an England regular and with a playing career lasting more than 30 years, Sir Stan only ever won one trophy: the FA Cup in 1953.

Alan Shearer, who would already be a knight if any of the royals were Geordies, was celebrating today in 1996 when he became the first man to hit 100 Premiership goals since its formation in 1992. He raised his right arm and wheeled away from goal in familiar fashion after scoring for Blackburn against Tottenham Hotspur in a 2-1 win for the reigning champions.

JANUARY 2

On this day in 1930 Jim Dyet pulled on a King's Park FC jersey for the first time and ran out on to the pitch at the Forthbank Stadium to make his debut for the now-defunct club against Forfar Athletic. Not only did King's Park destroy Forfar 12-2 but debutant Dyet opened his account in spectacular fashion, scoring eight times. This remains the highest-scoring debut in British football.

Staying in Scotland, today is also the anniversary of the second Ibrox Stadium disaster, which happened in 1971. Hundreds of fans were injured and 66 lost their lives when crush barriers collapsed as thousands of Rangers fans tried to leave the ground after Celtic took the lead in the 89th minute. Colin Stein scored an equaliser for Rangers during injury time and an initial theory that fans had tried to get back in to the ground when the goal went in was later discounted. The disaster remains the worst in the history of Scottish football.

JANUARY 3

Before the explosion of multimedia formats which allow you to check football results on television, the internet, your phone, watch or whatever comes next, the radio was the only place to hear all the day's scores. On this day in 1948 the familiar theme tune to *BBC Sports Report* was heard for the first time when the programme advertised as a 'new Saturday feature for sportsmen' was first broadcast. The show survives to this day – though they no longer read out the classified results, as producers reasoned fans now have plenty of other ways to check the scores.

Sir Alex Ferguson suffered his first-ever FA Cup third round defeat as Manchester United boss today in 2010. What made it worse was that it was bitter rivals Leeds United who inflicted defeat on Fergie's men. And what made it *even* worse was the fact that Leeds were licking their wounds in League One at the time. Jermaine Beckford's 19th-minute strike was enough to seal a stunning upset that is still sung about every week at Elland Road.

JANUARY 4

One of the most famous FA Cup giant-killings occurred on this day in 1992 when George Graham's Arsenal, the reigning league champions, visited the Racecourse Ground to play Wrexham, who were rock bottom of the entire league structure at the time, 92nd of 92 clubs. The Gunners were leading 1-0 with seven minutes left when Mickey Thomas and Steve Wadkin scored to win the tie for Wrexham in dramatic fashion.

Eleven years later and just over the border, Shrewsbury Town were emulating their Welsh counterparts today in 2003 when they knocked out Premier League side Everton, also by a 2-1 scoreline. The Shrews had lost their last two games 6-0 and 5-1 while Everton were in the early stages of the David Moyes revival, and the game was Wayne Rooney's first in the FA Cup. Nigel Jemson made light of the 80 league places separating the teams by scoring twice to give Shrewsbury a 2-1 win.

JANUARY 5

The all-conquering Liverpool side of the 1970s had a scare today in 1974 when Third Division Doncaster Rovers held them to a 2-2 draw at Anfield in the FA Cup third round. Kevin Keegan bagged both the Liverpool goals against his hometown club but Donny nearly won it in the final minute when they hit the woodwork. Liverpool won the replay 2-0 and went on to win the trophy.

Always a man with a penchant for the dramatic, it was on this day in 1997 that Keegan resigned as manager of Newcastle United. He had been lured back from the golf courses of Spain in 1992 to help the Magpies who were on their knees and heading for the Third Division. After saving them from relegation, getting them promoted and then taking them to the brink of the Premier League title in that famous 1995/96 season, KK decided he had had enough and left St James' Park, but not for the last time.

JANUARY 6

If you had to attribute Arsenal's position at the sharp end of English football to one man, it would have to be Herbert Chapman. He was a highly innovative coach who took an interest in every facet of the club. Shirt numbers, white footballs and games under floodlights were just some of Chapman's initiatives. He died on this day in 1934 of pneumonia after watching Arsenal's third team play Guildford City in pouring rain.

No doubt Coventry City were hoping Terry Butcher would have the same effect on the club as Chapman had at Arsenal when they hired him as their new player-manager in 1990. At 31 he was the youngest First Division boss but it was not to be and on this day in 1992 Butcher was shown the door at Highfield Road, and then told to get the hell out of it after a wretched run of results saw the Sky Blues stuck at the wrong end of the table.

KEVIN KEEGAN WAS NOT LOVING IT AT NEWCASTLE ANY MORE AND QUIT IN JANUARY 1997.

JANUARY 7

In a clear snub to Mrs Redknapp and their wedding day, Harry Redknapp claimed this was the best day of his life in 1984 when his Bournemouth side beat holders Manchester United 2-0 in the FA Cup third round at Dean Court. Under Big Ron Atkinson United had lost only one away game all season but were missing key defenders Gordon McQueen and Kevin Moran. They still had big names like Frank Stapleton, Bryan Robson and Norman Whiteside in the team and should have been more than enough to see off Harry's Third Division strugglers. They weren't.

There was more First Division embarrassment in the cup five years later in 1989 when Coventry City were knocked out by lowly non-league side Sutton United just two years after the Sky Blues had won the trophy. Sutton won the match 2-1 but their cup run was brought to a crashing halt in the next round when they were thumped 8-0 at Norwich.

JANUARY 8

When Cardiff City lined up to play Queens Park Rangers in an FA Cup tie in 1990 thousands of fans packed into Ninian Park hoping for a thriller. Sadly for them the game was a dull 0-0 draw but things got worse for Cardiff on this day, the Monday after the game, when club officials found canny thieves had broken in and stolen the £50,000 gate receipts from the game.

A less canny thief was in action on this day in 2003 when he chose perhaps the worst possible victim. Drug addict Carl Bishop broke into Duncan Ferguson's home but Big Dunc caught him at it, punched him and held on to the little tealeaf until the police arrived. In court, prosecutor Anthony Limont claimed: 'Mr Ferguson was very frightened,' but he's not fooling us. After Bishop's two-day hospital stay recovering from Big Dunc's own brand of justice he was given four years in prison.

JANUARY 9

On this day in 1900 Societa Podistica Lazio, or Lazio Track and Field Club was founded in the Prati district of Rome with the founding fathers naming the club after the district rather than the city to try to be inclusive to the whole region. They took up football a year later and had the Eternal City to themselves until 1927 when Roma were formed. Lazio resisted Mussolini's efforts to merge the two clubs, ensuring the fiercely contested Rome derby continues to this day.

The club had to wait until 1974 to win their first Scudetto, and their second was delivered in 2000 by Sven-Göran Eriksson, who resigned from the club on this day in 2001, clearing the way for him to become England manager. The Swede had agreed to take over in the summer but Lazio's form dived after his intention to quit was made public, forcing him to leave early to oversee England's rise to the heights of mediocrity.

JANUARY 10

Although Sir Alex Ferguson will always be remembered as the manager who brought through the 'Class of 92' golden generation of players at Old Trafford that included the likes of Beckham, Scholes and so on, he was also never afraid to splash the cash. On this day in 1995 he broke the British transfer record when he paid £6m plus Keith Gillespie for Newcastle striker Andrew Cole. Cole soon justified his fee and banged in plenty of goals for the Red Devils until he was sold to Blackburn in 2001.

Andrew's namesake Joe was part of another highly talented bunch of youngsters to come through the ranks together, this time at West Ham. Young Cole was just 17 when Harry Redknapp handed him his first league start at Old Trafford on this day in 1999. Even Joe's talents could not prevent the Hammers going down 4-1 to Manchester United.

January 11

Life was a beach for Charlton Athletic today in 2003 when they turned up at Stamford Bridge to play their Premiership fixture with Chelsea. The Addicks were soon undone by what Chelsea were laughably calling their pitch, which was made up entirely of sand with not a blade of grass in sight. Alan Curbishley said: 'It reminded me of a piece of land about to have a patio laid on it,' as his team went down 4-1.

Cultures clashed today in 2019, when a Leeds United intern was spotted observing a Derby County training session prior to the two sides' Championship clash. As Rams boss Frank Lampard fumed, Marcelo Bielsa causally admitted Leeds had been doing this all season before his team saw off Derby 2-0 at Elland Road. The tabloid press quickly dug their claws in, dubbing the incident 'Spygate'. Bielsa's brilliantly idiosyncratic response was to invite the media to a 90-minute press conference during which he laid bare the forensic details of all of his scouting and analytic methods, his point being that all this fuss over watching one meagre training session wasn't worth the bother.

January 12

Former World Footballer of the Year George Weah made his debut in English football today in 2000 after signing for Chelsea on a six-month loan deal. He came off the bench in his first game to score the winner against London rivals Tottenham at Stamford Bridge, having arrived in London from Italy just hours before the match. He said: 'It's a good beginning. I feel welcome. I'm hoping to do great things in London and I'm very happy that Gianluca [Vialli] believes in me.'

David Beckham announced a big-money move to the LA Galaxy on this day in 2007. The former England captain's deal with the MLS side was reportedly worth £128m but many people felt he was effectively consigning himself to semi-retirement in a below-par league. Despite leaving Real Madrid for the USA, Becks managed to win back his place in the England squad and help raise the profile of America's fourth-most-popular sport.

JANUARY 13

The only thing that perhaps gave Arsène Wenger greater pleasure than winning trophies was identifying and nurturing young talent. He did it many times at Arsenal, and on this day in 1997 he started a project that would go on to be one of his most successful when, as Monaco boss, he gave Thierry Henry his first professional contract. After an unsuccessful stint at Juventus, Henry followed his mentor to Arsenal, where a switch from winger to striker made him one of the best players in the world.

A young player that Wenger would have loved to get his hands on was Brazilian Alexandre Pato. AC Milan bagged the striker, nicknamed 'the Little Duck', for €22m from Internacional and today in 2008 he made his debut, getting on the scoresheet in the *Rossoneri*'s 5-2 win over Napoli at the San Siro.

JANUARY 14

Today in 1958 a crowd of 60,000 watched Manchester United beat Red Star Belgrade 2-1 in a European Cup tie at Old Trafford. The second leg, three weeks later, was to be the last appearance of the Busby Babes before the Munich disaster.

On the same day 11 years later, Sir Matt Busby announced he would retire as United manager at the end of the season. After rebuilding the team that was ripped apart by the tragedy in Munich, he had finally led United to the European Cup in 1968, ten years after the plane crash. He said: 'It's time to make way for a younger man... a track-suited manager.' Sir Bobby Charlton, who survived the crash and went on to win the European Cup, said at the time: 'Matt Busby's presence will always be at Manchester United. He is Manchester United.'

JANUARY 15

Today in 2006 Sven-Göran Eriksson was ruing the day he ever met Mazher Mahmood. The then-England boss thought he was a rich Arab sheikh interested in buying Aston Villa and installing Sven as manager but in reality the 'fake sheikh' was a *News of the World* reporter. Sven told him Rio Ferdinand was lazy, Wayne Rooney came from a poor family and most staggering of all, that he would quit England if they won the World Cup. If only Sven, if only.

"Remember the name: Wayne Rooney!" Clive Tyldesley told us when the Liverpudlian youngster scored that belter of a goal for Everton against Arsenal back in 2002. Today in 2021, Rooney announced his playing days were over and he would begin his managerial career as boss of Derby County. In between, Rooney had won every club trophy going with Manchester United – including five Premier League titles, the FA Cup and the Champions League – and become England's leading goalscorer.

JANUARY 16

Today in 1982 the draw for the upcoming World Cup in Spain turned into a right old Titus Shambles. Things got off to a bad start when they forgot to keep the seeded teams apart, and then one of the containers holding the balls jammed, splitting open and cascading ping-pong balls everywhere. Any hopes of FIFA salvaging any self-respect from the charade were dashed when the West German representative Hermann Neuberger accused the organisers of slave labour by using Spanish orphans to fetch the balls back and forth.

The 1982 World Cup was the only one that Kevin Keegan managed to play in, as England had not qualified for the two previous tournaments. Even then he only managed 26 minutes against Spain because of injury. Today in 2008 KK made a dramatic return as Newcastle manager, 11 years after resigning.

JANUARY 17

A Football League attendance record was set when 83,620 supporters gathered to watch Manchester United take on Arsenal today in 1948. The match was played at Manchester City's Maine Road stadium because Old Trafford was still undergoing reconstruction after suffering bomb damage in March 1941. It would not reopen until 1949. The match ended 1-1 and Arsenal went on to take the title. United were runners-up that season but did win the FA Cup – Matt Busby's first trophy for the club.

On this day in 2000, Frenchman Eric Cantona beat George Best to be named Manchester United's best player of the 20th century in a poll conducted on the club's official website.

JANUARY 18

By far the smallest crowd for any England match (reports vary from 85 to 300 fans) turned out at a snow-covered Kennington Oval on this day in 1879 to see the home side beat Wales 2-1 in the first meeting of the two sides on a football pitch. Herbert Whitfield of Old Etonians and Thomas Sorby of Thursday Wanderers put England 2-0 up before William Davies from Oswestry scored Wales' first ever goal in international football.

Jimmy Hill wasn't around in those days but the man who was a player, manager, club chairman, TV pundit and emergency linesman, was also the driving force behind the abolition of the maximum wage in football. Until Hill stuck his chin in, players could only earn a maximum of £20 a week, dropping to £17 in the summer. As chairman of the Professional Footballers' Association he had threatened a strike, but the Football League president Joe Richards backed down on this day in 1961 and within weeks Fulham's Johnny Haynes became the first £100-a-week player.

JANUARY 19

At Barcelona they throw pig's heads on to the pitch but Charlton's fans apparently prefer a more domestic animal missile. On this day in 1982 at the old Valley, the home fans livened up a 0-0 bore draw with Luton by lobbing the front half of a dead cat on to the pitch. Chris Weaver saw it happen: 'A passing policeman, who the cat had narrowly missed, nudged it gingerly to one side with his foot and that was that.'

Robbie Savage may be the pantomime villain of football but even he has probably never had a dead cat thrown at him. Today in 2005 he engineered himself a move from Birmingham City to Blackburn Rovers to hook up with his old international manager Mark Hughes. Rob claimed he wanted to move to be nearer his parents in Wales despite the fact Blackburn is just five minutes closer to Wrexham than Birmingham. Birmingham managing director Karren Brady said, 'If Robbie has come to that decision because of the distance between Blackburn and Wrexham, he should take a look on his map.'

JANUARY 20

Paolo Maldini began his extraordinary career on this day in 1985 when an injury to Milan defender Sergio Battistini in their game against Udinese gave the 16-year-old his first taste of first-team action. Following on from his father Cesare – who was a Milan player for 12 years – Paolo went on to become a legend for the *Rossoneri* in a one-club career that would see him win more trophies than you can shake a stick at. A stint as the club's technical director followed between 2018 and 2023 in which he helped deliver the club's first Serie A title for 11 years in 2022.

Theo Walcott wasn't even born when Maldini began his career but the young Englishman was making waves of his own today in 2006 when he became the most expensive 16-year-old in the history of British football with his transfer from Southampton to Arsenal, which was worth up to £12m.

JANUARY 21

After the Ridsdale and O'Leary era, administration, court cases and relegation from the Premier League, Leeds fans probably thought they had seen it all. There was still more to come, however, and on this day in 2005 the most controversial chairman in football bought control of the club. Ken Bates had sold Chelsea and was looking for a new project. The man once described by Martin O'Neill as 'a footballing cretin' made all the right promises about leading the club back into the Premiership. Instead another relegation and period of administration followed as things did not go to plan.

Tragedy struck today in 2021 when Argentine striker Emiliano Sala boarded a plane to travel to his new club Cardiff City, following his club-record £15m switch from Nantes. Sadly, he would never make it as his private plane – a Piper Malibu – crashed in the English Channel. Sala's body was recovered from the wreckage two weeks later. He was just 28 years old.

JANUARY 22

On this day in 1927 football began its long relationship with radio when former Harlequins rugby player Henry Blythe Thornhill Wakelam became the first ever radio football commentator. He described the action from a garden shed at Highbury as Arsenal and Sheffield United shared the points in a 1-1 draw, with Arsenal's Charlie Buchan scoring the first goal to be heard live on radio. *The Spectator* correctly predicted: 'That type of broadcasting has come to stay.'

Goodness knows what Wakelam would have made of events at Carrow Road on this day in 1963. An extremely harsh winter that year meant an FA Cup tie between Norwich and Blackpool had been postponed 11 times because of a frozen pitch, and in a desperate effort to get the game played the ground staff used a flamethrower to try to defrost the playing surface. It proved unsuccessful because as quickly as it was melted the ice froze again.

JANUARY 23

Great manager though he was, Sir Alex Ferguson made his fair share of expensive transfer gaffes. On this day in 2002 he blew £7.5m on Uruguayan striker Diego Forlán. Despite being thrown straight into the first team he had to wait a full eight months for his first goal, and even that was a penalty. Best remembered for taking his shirt off after scoring and then running around with it in his hands after failing to get it back on, he was moved on to Villarreal after just 10 goals in 63 league games for United.

On this day in 2005 Jermaine Pennant was arrested in Aylesbury after crashing a Mercedes into a lamp post while over the drink-drive limit. He was also serving a driving ban and was uninsured. Upon being arrested he had a cunning plan to evade punishment and reportedly told the arresting officer his name was Ashley Cole. Genius.

JANUARY 24

Leônidas da Silva, the Brazilian player known as the Black Diamond and top scorer at the 1938 World Cup, died today in 2004 at the age of 90. He was one of the first black players to play for the elitist Flamengo club and also had a chocolate bar named after him – Diamante Negro means Black Diamond in Portuguese and the bar is still produced in Brazil today. He is also credited as being one of the inventors of the bicycle kick although he claimed he was only perfecting the move invented by another Brazilian, Petronilho de Brito.

Unbelievably, former Aston Villa chairman Doug Ellis claims in his autobiography that he invented the bicycle kick, despite never having been a professional footballer. On this day in 2002 Deadly Doug saw yet another manager leave Villa Park on his watch when John Gregory resigned after nearly four years in charge, blaming 'the pressures of the job'.

JANUARY 25

French collar-turner-upper Eric Cantona stunned the world of football on this day in 1995 when he launched a kung-fu kick at Crystal Palace fan Matthew Simmons, who he claimed had been racially abusing him. He was banned for nine months, stripped of the French captaincy and initially sentenced to two weeks in prison, later reduced to 120 hours of community service. The incident preceded the bizarre press conference when Cantona's only words were: 'When the seagulls follow the trawler, it is because they think sardines will be thrown into the sea.'

In 1997 Trevor Sinclair produced a moment of brilliance even Cantona would have been proud of when he scored with a 35-yard overhead kick for Queens Park Rangers in an FA Cup tie at Loftus Road against Barnsley. His strike was good enough to win the *Match of the Day*'s Goal of the Season award.

JANUARY 26

Two of the game's great managers were born on this day. The first, in 1919, was Bill Nicholson. The Yorkshireman arrived at Tottenham when he was just 16 and save for a break for World War Two, he would serve the club as a player, coach and most famously, manager, for nearly 40 years. He oversaw Spurs winning a hatful of trophies including the league and cup double in 1961 – the first double of the twentieth century – as well as the European Cup Winners' Cup in 1963, making Spurs the first British winners of a European trophy.

That same year on this day, a future European trophy winner was born in Portugal. José Mourinho was famously Sir Bobby Robson's translator at Barcelona before really making his name at Porto where he won the European Cup. He went to Chelsea with a brief to deliver the same trophy but despite winning their first league title for 50 years, he could not succeed in Europe with the club.

JANUARY 27

A heated game between Arsenal and Liverpool at Highbury today in 2002 ended in three red cards being shown. Martin Keown was sent off first before Dennis Bergkamp was carded for a bad challenge on Jamie Carragher. In the aftermath a pound coin was thrown from the crowd at Carragher, who picked it up and hurled it straight back. He was immediately sent off. The incident cost him a £40,000 fine and earned him a three-match ban and a formal warning from the police.

Robbie Fowler, a long-time teammate of Carragher, made an emotional return to Anfield on this day in 2006 when Rafa Benítez re-signed him from Manchester City. The scouse striker had left in 2001, playing for Leeds and then City. He said: 'Since I have left, deep down I have always wanted to come back and it has been a long time but I'm glad to say I'm back now. Leaving was probably one of my biggest regrets I have had in football. I can't really believe it's happened again so I'm ecstatic to be honest.'

JANUARY 28

Denis Law was probably wondering why he even bothered on this day in 1961 when he scored six goals for Manchester City in an FA Cup fourth round tie at Luton. City were 6-2 up through Scotland's only Ballon d'Or winner Law, when the match was abandoned because of a waterlogged pitch. Law still scored in the replay five days later but Luton won the tie 3-1, rendering his earlier feat irrelevant.

Steve McManaman never scored six in a game, preferring to act provider for teammates like Robbie Fowler and Michael Owen at Liverpool, but on this day in 1999 he decided to turn his back on Anfield. He agreed to join Real Madrid on a free transfer when his contract expired at the end of the season. Labelled a Judas by Kopites, McManaman made the most of his time in Spain by winning La Liga and the European Cup twice.

JANUARY 29

Egypt provided England's opposition today in 1986 when two young players made their Three Lions' debuts. Southampton striker Danny Wallace was playing well at his club and scored the third goal in the 4-0 win in what would be his only England appearance. Peter Beardsley also made his debut that day when he came on for Gary Lineker and unlike Wallace, he would go on to play at the World Cup in Mexico later that year, and was a mainstay in the national side for ten years.

Another England player made his most important transfer move on this day in 1988. Arsenal manager George Graham paid Stoke City £350,000 to take Lee Dixon to Arsenal and the right-back quickly established himself as first choice in the best defence in the country. With George '1-0' Graham in charge it was a good time to be a defender at Arsenal as clean sheets were the priority and trophies aplenty followed.

JANUARY 30

Another Southampton striker was born on this day in 1951, and it was a good job he was for Saints fans. Bobby Stokes scored the winner when the Second Division club beat highly fancied top-flight team Manchester United 1-0 in the 1976 FA Cup final. Stokes won a car for being the first scorer in the match and rumour has it he started taking driving lessons before the game, fully expecting to score first and win the prize.

Future Southampton manager Glenn Hoddle was in hot water on this day in 1999 when comments he made to a journalist about disabled people were published in *The Times*. He said: 'You and I have been physically given two hands and two legs and a half-decent brain. Some people have not been born like that for a reason. The karma is working from another lifetime.' He was sacked four days later.

JANUARY 31

Before the multi-million pound contracts that footballers get these days, many found it a struggle to make ends meet when they retired and it was not unusual for a player to sell his medals to raise some much-needed cash for their retirement. Today in 1998 Tina Moore, ex-wife of Bobby Moore, announced she was to auction off his medals and trophies to raise £2m. England's only World Cup winning captain died of cancer in 1993, aged just 51.

Another England captain must have thought his international career was over today in 2008 when Fabio Capello left David Beckham out of his first England squad. At the time Becks was stuck on 99 caps and must have feared he would never be able to join the likes of Bobby Moore by gaining his century. Capello brought him into his next squad however, allowing Becks to reach his ton in a friendly 1-0 defeat to France in March 2008.

FOOTBALL
On This Day

JANUARY

February 1

Today in 2005, as Arsenal and Manchester United sized each other up before their top of the table match at Highbury, skippers Roy Keane and Patrick Vieira clashed in the tunnel when the Irishman took offence to his opposite number's posturing in front of Gary Neville. A blood and thunder match ensued, with United winning 4-2.

Two years later Arsenal were on the wrong end of another memorable Highbury encounter, when thanks to a series of Sol Campbell gaffes they were 2-0 down at half-time to West Ham. By the end of the interval the England defender had left the ground and went AWOL for several days, mulling over what Arsene Wenger would describe as 'a weakness in his life'. He returned ten weeks later, helping the Gunners to the European Cup final and booking his place in the England 2006 World Cup squad.

February 2

Stan Collymore played his last game of football today in 2001, turning out for Spanish side Real Oviedo. A player that the phrase 'inner demons' could have been invented for, Collymore's career was beset by a series of injuries, brushes with the law and downright stupidity. He has since been seen as a half-decent pundit and also, bizarrely, opposite Sharon Stone in *Basic Instinct 2*.

An England and Manchester United stalwart was also at the end of his playing road today in 2011 when Gary Neville announced his retirement at the age of 35. A club academy product and member of the famed 'Class of '92', Neville hung up his boots having played more than 600 times for United and won every club competition going, as well as winning 85 England caps. "I have been a Manchester United fan all my life and fulfilled every dream I've ever had," he said.

FEBRUARY 3

Like a Geordie Halley's Comet, Kevin Keegan was making one of his trademark sensational returns to Newcastle today in 1992, when he was appointed manager and tasked with avoiding relegation to the third tier. The Magpies were in a spot of bother and took a huge risk in flying Keegan into St James' after he had spent the last few years on golf courses across Spain, but it didn't turn out too badly for them.

Even those with a Keegan-esque sense of optimism would've struggled to get much out of today in 1940, when a record was set for the most postponements in Britain. The wartime league was hit by bad weather, with only one out of 56 matches beating the freeze but Bristol City would have wished that the fixture list was completely wiped out as they were thumped 10-3 by Plymouth.

FEBRUARY 4

As Roy Castle reminded us throughout our youth, if you want to be a record breaker, dedication's what you need. When Alan Shearer slotted home against Portsmouth today in 2006 his dedication paid off, as he became Newcastle's leading ever scorer, breaking 'Wor' Jackie Milburn's record of 200 goals that had stood since 1957. This was a far cry from the day that a young Shearer was placed in goal during his trial at the club as a 15-year-old – probably a move that Toon big-wigs regretted after they had to pay £15m to bring their favourite son home in 1996.

Meanwhile, down in London in 1991, Wimbledon Football Club had an audacious bid to play their home matches at Twickenham rejected by the Rugby Football Union. Quite why the Crazy Gang wanted to play in front of tens of thousands of empty seats is anyone's guess. A ground-share with Crystal Palace was the more sensible solution that emerged.

FEBRUARY 5

It took five postponements and a replay, but today in 1972 Hereford etched their name into the annals of FA Cup history when the non-league side defeated Newcastle United in their third round tie at Edgar Street. Ronnie Radford's 30-yard screamer is one of the FA Cup's most famous goals and will be familiar to anyone who's ever watched a *Match of the Day* FA Cup montage. Never one to belittle a fellow professional's achievements, Newcastle's England striker Malcolm Macdonald said: 'The ball hit a divot… Without that, it would've been a mis-hit and a throw-in to us.'

Hereford's day in the spotlight also marked the emergence of everyone's favourite sheepskin-wearing commentator, as the nation was treated to John Motson's overexcited recitation of statistics for the first time.

FEBRUARY 6

At 3.04pm on February 6 1958, British European Airways Flight 609 crashed on its third attempt to take off from a slush-covered runway at the Munich-Riem airport in what was then West Germany. The plane was carrying the Manchester United team that had just played a European Cup tie at Red Star Belgrade. Twenty-three passengers, including eight of Matt Busby's young side were killed, as the crash caused shockwaves around the world. With an average age of 23, the 'Busby Babes' had won the league title in 1956 and looked set to dominate English and European football for the next decade at least.

Another club facing an uncertain future on this day in 1986 was Hull City, who saw the locks at Boothferry Park changed by bailiffs under landlord David Lloyd's orders, as the club went to the brink of liquidation, before a takeover from former Leeds director Adam Pearson.

FEBRUARY 7

Successful, rich, hated by everyone but their own fans and full of overpaid pretty-boys – it was only going to be a matter of time until the ying of Manchester United met their yang in the New York Yankees. It was today in 2001 that United tried to emulate the Beatles and crack America, as they announced a joint marketing deal with the MLS giants. Yankee fever didn't really take over at Old Trafford, but if American foreign policy has taught us anything over the years, if they want something enough they'll take it, and two years later the controversial Glazer ownership of the club began.

By 2007 United had succumbed to the Glazers and on this day Liverpool fans were waking up with a pair of American owners as George Gillett and Tom Hicks had taken over the club. The dynamic duo promised loadsamoney, a new stadium and the Premiership trophy. Instead they delivered in-fighting, bickering, back-stabbing and mass protests from the Kop.

FEBRUARY 8

When they're not photoshopping England managers on to vegetables or banging on about immigration, the British tabloid press have occasionally been known to come up with a genuinely funny headline or two. The best in recent memory came after Inverness Caledonian Thistle shocked Celtic today in 2000, and *The Sun* went all Mary Poppins on us with: 'SUPER CALEY GO BALLISTIC, CELTIC ARE ATROCIOUS'. Proving that being a pundit wasn't the job he was worst at, John Barnes' managerial career came to a crashing halt after his expensively assembled Celtic squad went crashing out of the Scottish Cup.

In early 2012 the FA stripped John Terry of the England captaincy pending his trial for allegedly racially abusing Anton Ferdinand. Fabio Capello didn't agree with the decision and on this day, resigned as England manager in protest. Terry was eventually found not guilty, while the FA turned to Roy Hodgson to replace Capello, with the former Fulham and Liverpool boss spending four years in the job.

FEBRUARY 9

If you're interested in a cheaper, British version of Lee Majors' finest hour then read on. Today in 1979 Trevor Francis became the one million pound man, when Brian Clough broke the transfer record by snapping up Birmingham City's Trevor Francis for his Nottingham Forest side. To prevent this historic fee going to Trev's head, Clough insisted the fee was actually £999,999 – one pound short of the £1m mark, although after taxes the actual cost of the transfer was nearer £1.1m. When a European Cup-winning goal followed that season Cloughie was proved right to splash the cash.

New Wales manager Mark Hughes selected his first squad today in 2000 for a friendly away to Qatar. Ryan Giggs obviously fancied a trip to the desert, as he was drafted into the squad and made his first appearance in a friendly for nine years, helping his side win 1-0.

FEBRUARY 10

Back in 1929 La Liga was kicking off today, with Real Madrid getting the ball rolling with a 5-0 win over CD Europa. The Primera División was the brainchild of Jose Maria Acha and three of the ten founding teams have never been relegated: Real Madrid, Barcelona and Athletic Bilbao. Real's opening day joy was tempered by their rivals Barcelona, who pipped them to the inaugural title.

Another set of local rivals were clashing today in 2008 when an emotional Manchester derby was played out against the background of the 50th anniversary of the Munich air crash. After an impeccably observed silence for the victims of the disaster, City downed United 2-1, securing their first double in the league since the 1969/70 season. Not that it ended up doing City boss Sven-Göran Eriksson much good – he was sacked at the end of the season.

TREVOR FRANCIS BECAME THE FIRST £1M FOOTBALLER IN FEBRUARY 1979 WHEN HE SIGNED FOR BRIAN CLOUGH'S NOTTINGHAM FOREST.

February 11

In the run-up to France 98, English football's 'next big thing™' was Michael Owen. The fresh-faced 18-year-old made his England debut today in 1998 against Chile, becoming the youngest England player of the 20th century in the process. For all his youthful exuberance he couldn't prevent the Three Lions from suffering a 2-0 defeat at the hands of the South Americans.

Also tasting defeat were Manchester United, who suffered a heavy loss at the hands of Charlton Athletic today in 1939. The Addicks dished out a 7-1 drubbing at the Valley as United limped to a 14th place finish in the final season before Adolf Hitler's antics on the continent put the brakes on the league for a few seasons.

February 12

It was bound to happen eventually – after years of being beaten by Australia at cricket, tennis, rugby and every other sport you can think of, today in 2003 England were defeated by the Socceroos. The match in question was a friendly at West Ham's Boleyn Ground that saw England manager Sven-Göran Eriksson substitute his entire team at half-time. The Three Lions went down 3-1, with even perennial sick-note Harry Kewell getting on the scoresheet. Strewth!

One of the very few men to have actually won a trophy with England is goalkeeper Gordon Banks, who played every game of the Three Lions' successful 1966 World Cup campaign and made what is widely considered to be one of the best saves of all time when he denied Pelé at the 1970 World Cup. Former Leicester and Stoke City keeper Banks passed away on this day in 2019, aged 81.

FEBRUARY 13

Arsene Wenger showed his charitable side today in 1999, as he offered Sheffield United a replay of their fifth-round FA Cup clash following a controversial Marc Overmars winner. Kanu had latched on to a Ray Parlour thrown-in that was being returned to United keeper Alan Kelly following an injury to Lee Morris, but the Nigerian nipped in and squared to Overmars who duly scored.

Meanwhile, down on the south coast, fans' favourite Gordon Strachan quit as Southampton manager in 2004. Having saved the Saints from relegation in his first season in 2001 when the side found themselves second bottom of the Premiership, he established a settled side that even reached the UEFA Cup following their FA Cup final defeat to Arsenal in 2003. Paul Sturrock took over at St Mary's but would only last 13 games against a backdrop of player unrest and rumours that he was more interested in scoffing down his fried egg sandwiches than watching his team train.

FEBRUARY 14

Liverpool fans were mourning the passing of English football's most successful manager today in 1996, as Bob Paisley passed away aged 77. A product of the boot room era, Paisley had first joined Liverpool in 1939 and didn't leave the club until 1983, filling every job from centre-back to physiotherapist before he took over the hot seat from Bill Shankly. He would guide the Reds to 19 major honours, including their first three European Cups.

Two players not swapping Valentine's Day cards today in 2000 were Paul Gascoigne and George Boateng. Gazza added another self-inflicted injury to his long list when he went in to tackle Villa's Dutch midfielder and ended up breaking his own arm. Boro went down 4-0 and Gazza was given a misconduct charge from his friends at the FA as he continued to lunge from one crisis to the next.

FEBRUARY 15

There was a goal-fest at Highbury today in 1992 as the Gunners managed to put six past Sheffield Wednesday in a devastating 18-minute spell. With the game at 1-1 with 20 minutes left, Wednesday had one of the most spectacular implosions ever seen, as Kevin Campbell and Anders Limpar both bagged a brace, while Alan Smith, Paul Merson and Ian Wright all scored to consign the Yorkshire side to a 7-1 defeat. Wednesday would have the last laugh though, finishing one place above Arsenal in third when the season finished.

Anglo-Irish political tensions spilled over into the sporting world today in 1995 during England's game against the Republic of Ireland at Lansdowne Road. English hooligans rioted, tearing up seats and throwing them at the Irish fans. Referee Dick Jol, brother of former Tottenham manager Martin, had no choice but to abandon the game after only 27 minutes, with the Irish leading 1-0.

FEBRUARY 16

We all like to let ourselves go on our holidays, but today in 2000 the Leicester City squad, led by a certain Stanley Victor Collymore, took it to the max at the exclusive La Manga resort in Spain. Stan the Man, who had only been with the Foxes for a week, was fined two weeks' wages for spraying teammates, guests and staff with a fire extinguisher, ensuring that Leicester's mid-season break was in the headlines for all the wrong reasons.

Staying on foreign soil, Egypt were proud winners of the first ever African Nations Cup today in 1957 when the Pharaohs swept aside Ethiopia 4-0 with Mohamed Diab El-Attar bagging all four goals in the final. Only three teams took part in the fledgling competition, so whingeing British managers irked by losing half their players for the tournament were in the minority.

February 17

Today in 1940 Arsenal made their debut on the silver screen as *The Arsenal Stadium Mystery* was released. Manager George Allison and several players such as Cliff Bastin and Eddie Hapgood appeared in the film that centred around the poisoning of a rival player during a friendly between Arsenal and the Trojans, a fictional amateur side. Match action was provided for the film when Arsenal took on Brentford in the last game of the 1938/39 season, in what proved to be the Gunners' last game before the outbreak of World War II.

There was no doubt as to whodunnit at Arsenal today in 2007, as Cesc Fàbregas launched into a tirade of verbal abuse against Blackburn manager Mark Hughes. Following 90 minutes of the usual Rovers rough and tumble tactics, Cesc referred to the Welshman's time at Barcelona. 'That wasn't Barcelona football,' the youngster remarked, much to Hughes' chagrin.

February 18

Before they became a state-owned winning machine, Manchester City were not afraid of chopping and changing their managers at the drop of a hat. On this day in 1998 Joe Royle was the latest to fill the City hot seat, when he took over following Frank Clark's dismissal and became their sixth boss in 18 months. Although Royle couldn't put the brakes on City's slide into the third tier of English football, he was the man who brought them back up to the Premier League in 2000.

Meanwhile, Ireland today in 1882 became the fourth country to join the burgeoning international scene, as they played their first ever game against England at Knock Ground in Belfast. Ireland's heaviest ever defeat was witnessed by 2,500 fans, as England gave them a footballing lesson, handing out a 13-0 thrashing. Thanks to the efforts of 5-goal hero Howard Vaughton this remains England's record win.

FEBRUARY 19

Not many players have taken on Sir Alex Ferguson and won. Gordon Strachan, Jaap Stam, Dwight Yorke and Paul Ince will testify to this and a certain David Beckham was added to this list today in 2003, when Fergie kicked a boot at the England captain's face during a heated post-match team talk after United had been dumped out of the FA Cup by Arsenal. Both were keen to stress that the flying pair of size nines was an accident, but Becks was packing his bags to Madrid at the end of the season.

One player who saved himself from Fergie's hairdryer treatment was Alan Shearer, who turned United down more than once in his career. Today in 1992 he was more than likely catching the Scot's eye as his made his England debut, scoring in England's 2-0 win over France that saw Les Bleus suffering their first defeat in 20 games and artificially raising English expectations ahead of the European Championships.

FEBRUARY 20

Today's all about the good and then the bad of the beautiful game. In 1991 Liverpool and Everton contested one of the greatest ever Merseyside derbies, when their fifth round FA Cup tie ended up as a 4-4 extra time thriller. Everton had come from behind four times and ended up defeating their rivals 1-0 in a replay at Anfield.

Four years later football's dirty little secret reared its ugly head: bungs. A Premier League inquiry found Arsenal manager George Graham guilty of accepting an illegal payment from Norwegian agent Rune Hauge. The dodgy brown envelope in question featured a wad of fivers totalling £425,000 from the transfers of Pål Lydersen and John Jensen and was enough to see Graham immediately given the boot from Highbury and a worldwide year-long ban from the game.

FEBRUARY 21

Two weeks after the Munich disaster Duncan Edwards, the shining light of the Busby Babes, succumbed to his injuries as he died today in 1958, 15 days after the crash. Ask anyone of a certain age and they will tell you that the powerful wing-half was destined to be one of the greatest players England has ever produced. Bobby Charlton believed that his death was 'the biggest single tragedy ever to happen to Manchester United and English football.'

Mark Hughes was a worthy successor in the United line-up and he called time on his playing career today in 2000. Sparky had just taken over as the manager of the Welsh national side and wanted to focus all his efforts on securing more qualifying heartache for the Red Dragons.

FEBRUARY 22

Today in 1991 saw the fallout from the pulsating Liverpool derby we told you about two days earlier, as Liverpool boss Kenny Dalglish threw in the towel and announced his unexpected retirement from the game. King Kenny had brought three league titles and two FA Cups to the club to confirm his legendary status with Kopites everywhere. Like all too many 'retirements' he was back in the game 18 months later, this time spending Jack Walker's millions in Blackburn and delivering the league title.

It's thanks to the pioneering souls down at Fratton Park that we don't have to try and get through the working week without any football, as the first floodlit match was played at Portsmouth today in 1956. A problem with fuses meant that kick-off was delayed 30 minutes, but eventually Pompey played out a 2-0 win over Newcastle and football lodged itself further into the mainstream of popular culture.

FEBRUARY 23

Stanley Matthews, arguably the most famous English footballer of all time, died today in 2000. A true legend of the game, Matthews played top-flight football in England right up until his 50th birthday in his second spell at Stoke City, having also spent 14 years at Blackpool. Son of Jack Matthews, the boxer nicknamed the 'Fighting Barber of Hanley', 100,000 people lined the streets of Stoke for his funeral and his ashes were buried beneath the centre circle of the Britannia Stadium.

Claudio Ranieri was the unlikely architect of perhaps the most astonishing achievement in modern football when he led Leicester City to the Premier League title in 2016 – despite the Foxes having only just avoided relegation the previous year and being rated at 5,000-1 shots for the championship. But today in 2017, Leicester proved there's no room for emotion in football when they sacked the Italian just nine months after their greatest triumph. Dilly-ding, dilly-dong, Claudio.

FEBRUARY 24

Here's a lesson for football fans everywhere: never leave a game early. Today in 2004 Bournemouth striker James Hayter's family left Dean Court ten minutes early in order to catch a ferry back to the Isle of Wight, forgoing the climax of the clash against Wrexham. During this time however, the young Cherries striker came on as a sub and scored the fastest ever hat-trick in Football League history, bagging his treble in 2 minutes and 20 seconds as Bournemouth ran out 6-0 winners.

While there were only 5,899 in attendance that night, it was a different story up in Scotland as 134,461 descended upon Hampden Park today in 1968 for Scotland's European Championship qualifier against the English. The record crowd for a home international were treated to a 1-1 draw that saw England secure their place in the last eight of that summer's tournament.

February 25

Today in 2001 Liverpool showed signs of emerging from their mid-90s slump when they picked up their first piece of silverware for six years, winning the League Cup. Their opponents were First Division Birmingham City who took the scousers all the way to penalties, and this became the first ever English final to be settled by spot kicks.

In the 2007 League Cup final Chelsea and Arsenal played out a lively affair as the Millennium Stadium hosted its last English cup final before the new Wembley Stadium was finally ready. Didier Drogba's brace was enough to seal victory for the Blues after Theo Walcott scored his first goal for the Gunners in an incident-packed match that saw a lengthy stoppage after John Terry was knocked unconscious by the boot of Abou Diaby. An injury-time brawl saw Emmanuel Adebayor sent off as the bad-tempered clash reached its climax.

February 26

He possessed one of the greatest sets of sideburns to grace the game in an era when big hair was all the rage, and he wasn't too shabby on the pitch either. Former Arsenal and Tottenham goalkeeper Pat Jennings racked up his 1,000th appearance today in 1983. As a youngster, Jennings had never received any proper coaching, relying on a natural, if unorthodox technique that would see him fling his 6ft 2in frame around the goal, making sure his shovel-like hands kept out more than his fair share of shots. One of few players revered on both sides of north London, Jennings retired as Northern Ireland's most capped player with a whopping 119 appearances before Steven Davies broke his record in 2019.

Talking of international caps, Alan Shearer announced today in 2000 that after that summer's European Championships he would be calling it a day for England in order to concentrate on helping Newcastle United actually win something. That worked out well, hey Al?

FEBRUARY 27

We're going way back to turn-of-the-century Bavaria, where the German powerhouse Bayern Munich was formed today in 1900. Believe it or not, Germany's most successful football club started life as a gymnastics club. They've certainly come a long way since the days of somersaults and dives (no, we're not talking about Jürgen Klinsmann's spell there), as they can boast of having a trophy cabinet that contains more than 30 domestic league titles, six European Cups and every other trophy going.

Ninety-nine years later there was the birth of a less welcome part of football, as Sky Sports showed their first ever pay-per-view game. For only £7.95 every kick, throw-in and dodgy corner of Oxford United's First Division clash with Sunderland was yours. Unfortunately there were no goals for all those that splashed the cash, as the two sides played out a 0-0 draw.

FEBRUARY 28

If only it was still as easy to qualify for major tournaments as it was in 1930, England fans would have much less stressful lives. Way back then there was none of this two-year qualification lark, as FIFA simply invited the football world along. Today in 1930 was the deadline day for the first ever World Cup, with eight teams getting their forms in on time. England, believing themselves to be above this sort of thing, didn't bother.

Sir Alex Ferguson was receiving yet more plaudits on the back of his treble-winning season today in 2000 as he was awarded the Freedom of the City of Manchester. Fergie was the first person to receive the honour since Sir Matt Busby, who was handed the big key in 1967, a year before he conquered Europe with the Red Devils.

FEBRUARY 29

It took 128 years, but they got there eventually. Today in 2004 Middlebrough won their first ever major trophy, as the Teessiders defeated Bolton Wanderers 2-1 in a scrappy League Cup final at the Millennium Stadium. Remarkably both sides were managed by Englishmen, with Steve McClaren and Sam Allardyce pitting their wits against each other, meaning that the winner would be the first English manager to pick up a trophy since Brian Little won the League Cup with Villa in 1996. McClaren won out and the FA would get carried away by this a couple of years later.

On that same day Harry Kewell returned to Elland Road for the first time following his controversial move from Leeds to Liverpool. Kewell and his agent Bernie Mandic were rumoured to have pocketed £2m of the £5m transfer fee but whatever the truth, Kewell scored a peach of a goal in the 2-2 draw amidst a chorus of boos.

FOOTBALL
On This Day

MARCH

MARCH 1

The World Cup is the single biggest sporting event in the world as teams from all over the globe compete to win football's ultimate prize, or, in England's case, get knocked out at the quarter-finals. The man behind the competition was Frenchman Jules Rimet and it was on this day in 1921 that he became president of FIFA. He wanted to use football to bring countries closer together and his dream was realised in 1930 when the first competition was held in Uruguay.

A man who surely would have been a good bet for golden boot at the first World Cup had England taken part was Bill 'Dixie' Dean. The legendary Everton forward who once scored 60 league goals in one season died on this day in 1980 aged 73. Fittingly he passed away at Goodison Park watching his beloved Everton play Liverpool in the Merseyside derby.

MARCH 2

David Beckham's petulant kick at Diego Simeone at the 1998 World Cup got Becks sent off before England predictably went on to lose on penalties. It was on this day in 1999 that Simeone, the pantomime villain of the piece, admitted that he had conned the referee into red-carding Becks. He said: 'Let's just say the referee fell into the trap. You could say that my falling transformed a yellow card into a red card. Obviously, I was being clever. By letting myself fall, I got the referee to pull out a red card immediately.'

Beckham was again in the thick of the action on this day in 2003 when he lined up for Manchester United against Liverpool in the Worthington Cup final at the Millennium Stadium. Steven Gerrard scored Liverpool's first goal when his shot from 25 yards took a deflection off Beckham and looped over Fabien Barthez into the net. Michael Owen got the scousers' second and Jerzy Dudek put in a man of the match performance in goal to help Liverpool to a 2-0 win over their rivals.

MARCH 3

Local derbies are the most intense matches there are and with bragging rights up for grabs for the victors and heartache for the losers, there is nothing better than beating your nearest neighbours. On this day in 1918 in the Derby della Madonnina between Internazionale and AC Milan, the red and black half of Milan was revelling in an 8-1 thrashing of Inter.

Back in England and ten years later on the same day a young Ronnie Dix was making history of his own when he became the youngest goalscorer in Football League history. Dix was 15 years and 180 days old when he scored for Bristol Rovers.

MARCH 4

Today in 1967 QPR pulled off one of the greatest comebacks of all time to win the League Cup in the first final to be held at Wembley. Rangers went into the game massive underdogs against West Brom who were two divisions above them at the time and went into a first half 2-0 lead. In the second half Roger Morgan and Rodney Marsh levelled the score before the appropriately-named Mark Lazarus scored with less than ten minutes to go to bring the Hoops back from the dead.

If that match was a thrilling contest that could have gone either way, the match played on this day in 1972 between Leeds and Southampton was about as one-sided an affair as is possible between two professional teams. 'A performance which flowed like poetry,' one newspaper said as Leeds thrashed Saints 7-0. 'We'd already scored six and felt sorry for them,' Peter Lorimer would claim, although there was no mercy from the Leeds players who back-flicked and showboated their way through the game while Ted Bates' Southampton players chased shadows. A Lorimer hat-trick, a brace from Allan Clarke and goals from Mick Jones and Jack Charlton did not flatter the hosts.

MARCH 5

While football clubs have now become the latest must-have accessory for international billionaires, British businessmen took an interest a long time ago. On this day in 1993 porn baron David Sullivan proved he was a fan of all things blue when he bought Birmingham City. The owner of the *Sunday Sport* and *Daily Sport* newspapers and sometime porn film producer snapped up the St Andrew's club after his first love West Ham snubbed him when, despite being a major shareholder, he was not invited to join the board. He later sold Birmingham and bought West Ham.

Today in 2000 a footballer-turned-actor proved that he could still play a bit when he scored a hat-trick on his debut for his new club. Stan Collymore broke his leg soon after his first Leicester appearance and only ever scored two more goals for the club.

MARCH 6

On this day in 1967 Accrington Stanley, the club made famous by a milk advert from the 1980s, became the first league club to resign from the competition mid-season. A creditors' meeting the day before revealed the club owed £62,000 and the directors concluded the club was bust. The *Accrington Observer* ran with the headline: 'STANLEY – THE END'. Days later a man walked into the club's office with £10,000 he wanted to lend them interest free but league secretary Alan Hardaker decided to accept the directors' original letter of resignation and the club was dead. Their last match had been a 4-0 loss to Crewe Alexandra.

Another club having problems on this day in 2006 was Sunderland. Chairman Bob Murray sacked manager Mick McCarthy who, despite steering the club to promotion in 2005 as First Division champions, managed just two wins while in the Premiership. The club was relegated with a record low of 15 points and three wins which beat their own record, set in 2003, of 19 points. Derby have since 'bettered' that with their paltry 11 points in the 2007/08 season.

BOBBY MOORE LEFT WEST HAM FOR FULHAM IN 1974 (SEE OVER).

MARCH 7

Dennis Viollet was one of the lucky survivors of the Munich air crash that destroyed the Busby Babes Manchester United team. Viollet went on to score 178 goals for the Old Trafford club and formed a prolific partnership with Tommy Taylor. In ten years at the club between 1952 and 1962 he made 291 appearances and won two England caps but on this day in 1999 he died at home in the USA, aged 65, from a brain tumour.

Sir Bobby Charlton was another famous survivor of the crash and he was later knighted for his part in England's World Cup win in 1966. Today in 2000 the Queen finally honoured the five 'forgotten' members of the team who played at Wembley on that historic day. Nobby Stiles, Alan Ball, Roger Hunt, Ray Wilson and George Cohen all received MBEs at Buckingham Palace.

MARCH 8

Eight years after he had led England to their finest triumph in the World Cup final Bobby Moore's career was on the wane and today in 1974 West Ham did what would have once been unthinkable, and put Moore up for sale. His last match for the Hammers had been an FA Cup tie with Hereford. He joined Second Division Fulham and ended up facing his old club West Ham in the FA Cup final at Wembley in his first season at Craven Cottage. He could not prevent West Ham winning 2-0.

Moore was one of the first players to realise the commercial aspect of football and memorably starred in an advert for pubs encouraging people to 'look in at the local' but even he could not have foreseen how much money would one day be sloshing around the game. Today in 2000 Manchester United became the first £1bn club after the share price rose to see the club valued at £1.02bn.

MARCH 9

FC Internazionale Milano, now one of the biggest clubs in the world, was founded on this day in 1908. The club's origins lie in their great rivals AC Milan when it was known as Milan Football and Cricket Club. Some foreign members of the club were unhappy about the dominance of Italians in the football team and so split off to form their own team with their choice of name reflecting their open-to-all policy.

Inter provided the opposition when Jock Stein led Celtic to the European Cup in 1967 – the first British club to win it – and it was on this day that Stein was given the manager's job at Celtic Park. When he took over, the club had gone eight years without a trophy but he won the Scottish Cup in his first season and went on to guide the Glasgow giants to 11 league titles and a hatful of cups in his 13 years in charge.

MARCH 10

Despite being seen as the poor relations to the rest of the European football family, Greece did ruffle a few feathers in 2004 when they were crowned European champions. Olympiacos, their most famous and successful club side, were founded today in 1925 in the Piraeus suburb of Athens. Known as Thrylos (meaning legend), the club plays in the gloriously named Derby of the Eternal Enemies (also known as the Mother of all Battles) against cross-town rivals Panathinaikos.

Although he was there for a long time, David O'Leary's spell at Arsenal does not quite count as an eternity. On this day in 1992 the Irish centre-half made his 700th appearance for the Gunners. After making his debut as a fresh-faced 17-year-old against Burnley in 1975, O'Leary spent 18 years at Highbury and still holds the record for the most appearances (722) and the most league appearances (558) for the north London club.

MARCH 11

On this day in 1941 German bombing destroyed much of Old Trafford, including the main stand. Designed by famous stadium architect Archibald Leitch and opened in 1910, the ground had to be closed for nearly ten years while it was rebuilt. In the meantime Manchester United had to play their home games at Manchester City's Maine Road ground. The first game at the newly reopened stadium was on August 24 1949, a 3-0 victory over Bolton Wanderers.

Today in 1963 Blackburn versus Middlesbrough, the last of the FA Cup third round games was finally completed, nine weeks after it was first scheduled to be played because of the so-called 'Big Freeze'. The extremely harsh weather saw Britain covered in snow for 67 days, throwing sports meetings everywhere into chaos. No fewer than 16 games were postponed ten or more times and the Lincoln versus Coventry match was called off 15 times. In all, there were no fewer than 261 postponements in the FA Cup third round alone.

MARCH 12

Rotund goalkeeper Neville Southall was back in action between the sticks today in 2000 when he turned out for Bradford City in their Yorkshire derby match with Leeds aged 41. He was called up to play after regular 'keeper Matt Clarke had injured himself falling down the stairs. Big Nev, never the most streamlined of goalies, had let himself go a tad. One match report said: 'I'm sure if he turned up on a Sunday morning for my team, we'd turn him away for being too fat.' Bradford lost 2-1.

Howard Wilkinson was appointed Sunderland manager after Peter Reid's sacking in October 2002, but after a run of just two wins in 20 games Wilkinson was sacked and, on this day in 2003, Mick McCarthy was given the job of keeping the club in the Premiership. He couldn't, but kept his job and won promotion as champions the following season.

MARCH 13

Queen's Park, the first Scottish club to be formed, were finding life a little lonely – even resorting to taking part in the English FA Cup, and reaching the final twice – because of the lack of local competition. Keen to remedy this, the club placed an advert in a local newspaper and were joined for a meeting in the Dewar's Hotel in Glasgow by representatives from Clydesdale, Vale of Leven, Dumbreck, Third Lanark, Eastern and Granville. Kilmarnock sent their apologies, but the eight clubs agreed to form the Scottish Football Association on this day in 1873.

Today in 2020 the Covid-19 pandemic hit football and it was announced that all domestic games had been postponed until at least April 4. As it turned out, it would be June 17 before football restarted in England, with Aston Villa vs Sheffield United and Manchester City vs Arsenal the first two matches of 'Project Restart'.

MARCH 14

Blackburn Rovers were the first club to have won the Premier League and later relegated from it, but today in 2000 they appointed Graeme Souness as the manager who would lead them back to England's top tier. Souness came in after the Brian Kidd experiment had failed with the club struggling in the First Division. Souness won promotion in 2001 and won the League Cup the following season before leaving for Newcastle in 2004.

David Moyes arrived at Goodison Park on this day in 2002 with the club struggling at the wrong end of the table under Walter Smith. Moyes soon steered the club to safety and then pushed Everton up the league and transformed them from relegation candidates into European contenders on a tight budget.

MARCH 15

Trivia fans will already know that Everton initially played their home matches at Anfield but in 1892 the club had a disagreement with the stadium owner John Houlding about rent and left to build their own ground, Goodison Park. Faced with an empty stadium with no team, Houlding decided to start his own club and, on this day that year Liverpool FC was born. The club who were only created to fill a stadium were league champions by 1901.

Swindon Town were formed 13 years before Liverpool but it took them 90 years to win their first major trophy. On this day in 1969 the Third Division side were extreme underdogs to First Division Arsenal in the League Cup final. Eight Arsenal players were sidelined with flu and a badly cut-up and wet Wembley pitch played into Swindon's hands as the Wiltshire side won 3-1 after extra time.

MARCH 16

On this day in 1972 the first ever FA Cup final took place at the Kennington Oval in London. Wanderers, captained by FA secretary and inventor of the competition Charles Alcock, beat the Royal Engineers 1-0 thanks to a goal from Morten Betts who was playing under the pseudonym 'A H Chequer'. Just 2,000 spectators watched the match in which Lieutenant Edmund Creswell of the Royal Engineers broke his collarbone after just ten minutes, although incredibly he continued playing.

Less serious injuries caused controversy on this day in 2002 when a First Division match between Sheffield United and West Bromwich Albion had to be abandoned after 82 minutes when the home team were left with only six players on the pitch. The Blades had three players sent off and were losing 3-0 when two more went off injured. West Brom boss Gary Megson accused United manager Neil Warnock of faking the injuries to engineer a replay. The FA fined the Blades £10,000 and awarded the three points to West Brom, but Warnock was cleared of any wrongdoing.

MARCH 17

Most clubs have at least one manager who is seen to define them and who spearheaded their most successful times. For Leeds United this man is undoubtedly Don Revie and on this day in 1961 he was appointed as manager at Elland Road. Then in the Second Division, Revie soon had Leeds promoted and depending on your point of view, his side became the most feared/respected/talented/dirty team of the 1960s and 1970s. By the time he left to manage England in 1974 he had won two league titles, one FA Cup, one League Cup and two Fairs Cups.

Revie had left the England job by the time Diego Maradona was tormenting the Three Lions for Argentina but it was on this day in 1991 that Maradona's own decline began. By this time a cocaine addict, he failed a random drugs test while playing for Napoli and was banned for 15 months. He never played in Italy again and after a brief spell at Sevilla after his ban ended, he returned to Argentina to play out the remainder of his career.

MARCH 18

One of the world's greatest and most iconic clubs was formed today in 1900 when Floris Stempel, Carel Reeser and brothers Han and Johan Dade together founded AFC Ajax. Under manager Rinus Michels the club played 'Total Football' with the inspirational Johan Cruyff leading them on the pitch as they won just about every trophy going, even winning the European Cup three times in a row from 1971 to 1973.

Bradford City do not quite have the pedigree of Ajax but they have had their moments, most notably lifting the FA Cup in 1911. Today in 2000 was not such a halcyon day for the club when they lost 4-0 to Coventry at Highfield Road. Despite the heavy defeat which left the club in the bottom three of the Premiership, manager Paul Jewell masterminded a great escape which saw them stay up on the last day of the season.

MARCH 19

One of the consequences of Swindon's victory in the 1969 League Cup was the creation of another competition called the Anglo-Italian Cup. It was created because Swindon's Third Division status meant they were denied entry into the Fairs Cup. It had a complicated qualification format and pitted teams from England and Italy's lower divisions against each other. On this day in 1995 Notts County lifted the trophy after beating Ascoli at Wembley, watched by just 12,000 fans.

On this day in 1998 Paul Gascoigne left Glasgow Rangers and signed for Middlesbrough for £3.4m, just five months after he claimed he would never return to English football. In November 1997 he said: 'Whatever happens, Rangers will be my last club in Britain. If I do leave Rangers it won't be for another club in Britain. I can't see myself playing in the Premiership.'

MARCH 20

Football was coming home in 1966 when England hosted the World Cup. Prior to the event the Jules Rimet trophy itself was on display in London when it was stolen on this day. With very little in the way of any leads the FA commissioned a replica to be made in secret so they would have something to hand over come the June competition. In the end a small dog named Pickles succeeded where the whole of the Metropolitan Police Force failed when he found the trophy wrapped in newspaper under a hedge in south London seven days later.

At the tournament itself legendary goalkeeper Lev Yashin was between the sticks for the USSR team that reached the semi-finals. Nicknamed the Black Spider, Yashin is the only goalkeeper to have won the Ballon d'Or, and he saved more than 150 penalties in his career. Awarded the Order of Lenin in 1967, Yashin died on this day in 1990.

MARCH 21

Two years after the first FA Cup final in England was played, the Scottish Football Association Challenge Cup, or the Scottish Cup as it is better known, was created, modelled on the English competition. On this day in 1874 the first final was won by Queen's Park who defeated Clydesdale 2-0 in front of 3,000 fans. Billy MacKinnon and Robert Leckie scored for the Glasgow team which is the oldest club in Scotland, having been founded in 1867.

More than one hundred years later and another Scot was lifting a different trophy in triumph. On this day in 1999 Tottenham Hotspur won the League Cup after defeating Leicester City 1-0 at Wembley. An Allan Nielsen goal in injury time was enough to win the club's first honour for eight years and it was masterminded by George Graham, although it still did not endear the former Arsenal man to the Spurs faithful.

MARCH 22

A Scotsman was also the brains behind the English Football League. Aston Villa director William McGregor decided a properly structured system of games was needed to help clubs organise their finances properly. McGregor wrote to several leading clubs proposing his idea and on this day in 1888 twelve clubs met at Anderson's Hotel in Fleet Street, London to discuss the idea. The league was born and the first matches were played later that year.

Not even McGregor could have foreseen how far the English game would develop and on this day in 2000 Chelsea became the first Premiership side to field an all-foreign team in a European match. Manager Gianluca Vialli left Dennis Wise on the bench but the foreign legion stuttered against Lazio in the Champions League group match, losing 2-1. The result ended Chelsea's unbeaten home run in European competition which stretched back to 1958 – 33 games in all.

MARCH 23

Nettie Honeyball may sound like the name of the squeeze in a James Bond film but she was actually the early driving force behind women's football and it was on this day in 1895 that the first official women's match in England took place between a northern and southern XI. The northern team won the match 7-1 and the women's game grew in popularity over the next 20 years until the FA, worried about the impact on the men's game, banned women from FA pitches in 1921.

England opened their Euro 2024 qualifying campaign with a 2-1 win against Italy on this day in 2023. It was England's first away win in Italy since back in 1961 – but more noteworthy was the fact that Harry Kane scored a first-half penalty. It was his 54th goal for the Three Lions – meaning he beat Wayne Rooney's total to become England's all-time record goalscorer.

MARCH 24

While simulation, or cheating as it should be called, has now become common in top-level football there are rare examples of fair play among players. On this day in 1997 Robbie Fowler appeared to go down under a challenge from David Seaman. He was awarded a penalty but pleaded with referee Gerald Ashby not to give it claiming he had not been touched by the goalkeeper. Seaman saved Fowler's spot kick but Jason McAteer scored from the rebound. It was widely thought that Fowler missed on purpose and he won a UEFA Fair Play Award for his honesty but he said afterwards: 'I tried to score. I never missed on purpose. It just happened, it was a bad penalty.'

One person who did score ten years after Rob's miss was Giampaolo Pazzini. On this day in 2007 the young Italian became the first person to score a goal in the rebuilt Wembley Stadium in an under-21 match between England and Italy. Pazzini scored a hat-trick in the 3-3 draw.

MARCH 25

On this day in 1992 another lower league club lost their perpetual fight for existence when Aldershot FC folded and became only the second club after Accrington Stanley to resign from the league mid-season. Two years earlier 19-year-old property developer Spencer Trethewy appeared to have saved the club when he promised £200,000 of investment. The only trouble was he did not have it and the club went bust. Aldershot Town FC was formed shortly afterwards to keep football in the town.

More dodgy directors were ousted on this day in 2003 when fans of York City got together and raised enough money to take over their club and rescue it from the brink of extinction. In 2001 former chairman Douglas Craig was threatening to withdraw from the league unless someone bought him out, and the next chairman John Batchelor was no better, doing little except change their name to York City Soccer Club. The *York Evening Press* hailed the fans as: 'A remarkable body of men and women. From the Trust's astonishingly successful launch to its takeover of the club, they have played a blinder.'

MARCH 26

When he wasn't pushing over referees or making fascist salutes, Paolo di Canio was a top player capable of sublime skill and on this day in 2000 he scored a beautiful volley for West Ham against Wimbledon. Trevor Sinclair crossed to the far left of the area to find the Italian, who struck his volley with the outside of his right foot from 12 yards out. It was voted goal of the season and one of the top ten goals of a decade of the Premiership in 2002.

Another player remembered for scoring top-quality goals is David Beckham and after weeks of will he/won't he speculation in the press, new England manager Fabio Capello proved there is still room for sentiment in the modern game by handing Beckham his 100th England cap in a friendly against France on this day in 2008.

MARCH 27

There is an unwritten rule that when a new manager takes over, a win in their first game is a must. Kevin Keegan was only appointed on a temporary basis as England boss in 1999 but he got the winning start demanded on this day when England beat Poland 3-1 in a Euro 2000 qualifier at Wembley with Paul Scholes scoring a hat-trick. England went on to clinch qualification via a play-off with Scotland.

In 2002 Scotland decided to follow England's lead and appointed their first ever foreign manager, Berti Vogts. The German was not blessed with the talent in his squad that his England counterpart was and on this day in 2002, in Vogts' first match in charge, the Scots were thrashed 5-0 by a rampant French side in a friendly in Paris. Vogts refused to be too downhearted by the result and said: 'We have to look to the next game and I am sure we will play better.'

MARCH 28

With Swiss London Underground enthusiast Christian Gross in charge, Spurs were struggling at the wrong end of the table in 1998 but on this day they went some way to securing their survival thanks to a 3-1 win at Crystal Palace. Jürgen Klinsmann bagged the third goal.

Gross was sacked soon after and former Arsenal boss George Graham brought in but the White Hart Lane faithful could never forgive or forget his Gunners past and he was given the heave-ho in 2001. His replacement was Spurs hero Glenn Hoddle who left his previous job at Southampton on this day to take over at Tottenham. Never one to keep quiet, Saints chairman Rupert Lowe was not best pleased about Hoddle's defection. He said: 'I was disappointed that Glenn had chosen to turn his back on the club that gave him the opportunity to resume his career in top-flight management and on a squad which he had welded into an exciting team.'

MARCH 29

William 'Billy' Townley made his name on this day in 1890 when he became the first man to score a hat-trick in an FA Cup final. In those pre-Wembley days the final was played at the Kennington Oval and Townley's Blackburn Rovers team thrashed Sheffield Wednesday 6-1 to lift the cup that year. There have only been two final hat-tricks since, James Logan for Notts County in 1894 and Stan Mortensen in 1953.

More accustomed to trying to prevent hat-tricks than score them, David James made his England debut on this day in 1997. Then with Liverpool, James kept a clean sheet at Wembley as England beat Mexico 2-0 thanks to goals from Teddy Sheringham and Robbie Fowler. James would have to wait another five years before he was England's first choice number one, playing understudy to David Seaman until 2002.

MARCH 30

Manchester United and Arsenal began one of football's biggest rivalries on this day in 1895, when they met each other under their former guises of Newton Heath and Woolwich Arsenal long before Messrs Ferguson and Wenger started playing mind games with each other. The two sides met at Arsenal's early Manor Ground home and it was the Gunners that drew first blood, winning 3-2 in their Second Division clash.

Nearly 100 years later one of United's greatest ever players was in trouble after some unsavoury actions at Elland Road. In rather a tame warm up to his later kung-fu exploits, Eric Cantona returned to play at Leeds with Manchester United and spat at one of the home fans. Today in 1993 he was fined a typically paltry £1,000 for his actions, no doubt with a stern warning to behave himself which evidently fell on deaf ears.

MARCH 31

Arsenal and England midfielder David Rocastle passed away on this day in 2001 at the tragically young age of 33 from non-Hodgkin's lymphoma. Rocky, as he was known by the Highbury faithful, broke into the Gunners first team in 1985 and went on to become an Arsenal legend, making 277 appearances and scoring 34 goals. His weaving runs, ball control and inspiration played a key part in the Gunners side that picked up a League Cup in 1987 and two league titles in 1989 and 1991. Author, Arsenal fan and list enthusiast Nick Hornby ranked Rocky's winner against Spurs in the 1987 League Cup semi as one of his all-time top five football moments, which is no mean feat.

It in unlikely Hornby views the match Arsenal played today in 2007 with such affection. Taking on Liverpool at Anfield, the Gunners lost 4-1 with disproportionate striker Peter Crouch scoring a perfect hat-trick: one with each foot and a header.

FOOTBALL
On This Day

APRIL

APRIL 1

History was made today in 1990 when the first-ever match was broadcast on satellite television in Britain. Arriving ten months behind schedule, British Satellite Broadcasting (BSB) introduced us to the commentary of Martin Tyler and Andy Gray, who described the action as Rangers rode out a 3-0 victory at home to Old Firm rivals Celtic. The early days of satellite television were a chaotic affair, with Rupert Murdoch's Sky TV merging with BSB in November 1990, paving the way for the formation of the Premier League 18 months later.

Wendy Toms became the first female referee to be added to the Football League's list of officials today in 1995. Toms worked her way up the leagues as an assistant referee, culminating in her running the line in the 2000 League Cup final between Leicester City and Tranmere Rovers.

APRIL 2

When Graeme Souness was appointed Newcastle manager he took over from Sir Bobby Robson with a brief to instil discipline in a squad that was seen as badly in need of a kick up the backside. Graeme proved he was clearly losing the battle on this day in 2005 when Lee Bowyer and Kieron Dyer decided to have a fist fight right in the middle of a match at St James' Park. Players from Newcastle and opponents Aston Villa stepped in to pull the pair apart before they both received their marching orders.

Venturing even further north, there was another frustrated set of fans today in 2000 as Celtic had a remarkable four goals disallowed in a 17-minute spell against Kilmarnock. Tommy Johnson had particular beef, bagging a hat-trick that never was, although his side still managed a 4-2 win.

ROBBIE FOWLER WAS IN TROUBLE AGAIN AFTER HIS GOAL-LINE SNIFFING CELEBRATION IN APRIL 1999 (SEE OVER).

APRIL 3

Robbie Fowler was in a spot of bother today in 1999; the cheeky scouser had to apologise for one of his more controversial goal celebrations during a Merseyside derby. After bagging an equaliser from the spot, Fowler got on his hands and knees and began sniffing the white line of the penalty area – a response to the near-constant accusations of drug use he faced from rival fans throughout his career. Although the referee took no action during the 3-2 win for Liverpool, the club took a dim view of the incident and fined him £64,000.

One player who didn't need to pretend that he was off his face was Diego Maradona. The Argentine legend's beloved club Boca Juniors were formed by a group of young Italian immigrants on this day in 1905.

APRIL 4

Today in 1982 Lancashire side Darwen suffered a 12-0 loss against West Brom. This score was matched by Nottingham Forest in their 1909 trouncing of Leicester Fosse and remains the record defeat in English top-flight history.

History was made on this day in 1953 when Duncan Edwards made his Manchester United debut in a 4-1 defeat to Cardiff City. At 16 years and 185 days old, Edwards became – at the time – the youngest player ever to feature in the top flight of English football. Often described as the most talented of the Busby Babes – if not the most talented English player of his generation – Edwards was tragically killed in the Munich air disaster when he was just 21. By then he'd already played more than 150 times for United, and won 18 senior England caps.

APRIL 5

Two Leeds United fans were killed today in 2000 on the eve of Leeds' UEFA Cup clash against Galatasaray in Istanbul. Christopher Loftus and Kevin Speight had travelled to Turkey for the semi-final first leg but trouble broke out between two sets of fans the night before the match in one of football's most shameful and tragic episodes. As Aston Villa manager John Gregory said at the time: 'You don't go to a football match and expect not to come home.'

Today in 1947 Rangers won the first ever Scottish League Cup, as the Southern League Cup was rebranded after its war-enforced suspension. The Gers were 4-0 winners over Aberdeen, thanks to goals from Torrance Gillick, William Williamson and a brace from James Duncanson and soon added the league title to their trophy cabinet that season.

APRIL 6

Today in 1994 the FA moved quickly to avoid a PR disaster as they hastily cancelled England's friendly against Germany that was scheduled for April 20. History buffs everywhere will know that this happens to be Adolf Hitler's birthday and when English intelligence discovered that mass protests were being arranged to coincide they called off the match.

In 2006 Manchester United were going all Gordon Gekko on us, as chief executive David Gill declared that they wanted a slice of the forthcoming World Cup profits. Gill had his eyes on a piece of the £636m profit that the 2002 tournament made, deciding that it would be better in the Old Trafford coffers rather than going back into the game and being distributed amongst national associations and to finance FIFA's charitable activities. Thankfully, common sense won out in the end, a rarity for football's governing body as Gill went home empty handed.

APRIL 7

Hapless Frenchman Alain Perrin began his eight-month spell as Portsmouth manager today in 2005. Drafted in after Harry Redknapp had jumped ship to Southampton, Pompey fans were worried from the start after he admitted in his first press conference that he knew nothing about his next-day opponents, Charlton. Even with the helping hand of 'consultant' David Pleat, Perrin was unable to make his mark on English football, lasting until November when 'Arry decided he was a Skate, not a Saint, and returned to the club.

It was happy days up in Sunderland today in 1973 as the unfancied Second Division side booked their place in the FA Cup final, defeating Arsenal 2-1 in the semi at Hillsborough. Under the management of Bob Stokoe, the Mackems would cause one of the greatest FA Cup upsets of all time, defeating the all-conquering Leeds United in the final at Wembley.

APRIL 8

It is the one thing all professional footballers fear more than anything else – sustaining a career-ending injury. It was on this day in 1996 that Coventry defender David Busst had his playing days cut short when he broke his leg during a match. The break was so bad that, with bone protruding from his skin, it looked as if he might even need to have his leg amputated at one point. Some 26 operations later and although doctors saved his leg, they couldn't save his career and he was forced to hang up his boots at the age of 29.

Wycombe Wanderers' epic FA Cup run came to an end today in 2001 when the giant-killers met their match against Liverpool in the FA Cup semi-final at Villa Park, going down 2-1.

APRIL 9

International football should be the most exciting and glamorous time in any player's career – the pinnacle of achievement in their profession. On this day in 2001 Tonga's finest found out it can also be a harsh and unforgiving world of crushing defeats that would never occur in any other football environment when Australia defeated the plucky little islanders 22-0. The score was a new record in international football, but would only stand for two days before the Aussies were at it again, this time picking on American Samoa and notching up 31 unanswered goals.

Also among the goals today in 1988 was a young lad by the name of Alan Shearer. The 17-year-old Southampton striker became the youngest ever to bag a top-flight hat-trick, breaking a 30-year record held by Jimmy Greaves. Not too shabby, seeing as it came on his full debut and his opponents were George Graham's famously stingy Arsenal side.

APRIL 10

Living in the spotlight of a bigger, more glamorous and more successful cross-city rival is never easy, and perhaps that's why Atlético Madrid went off the rails today in 1974 during their European Cup semi-final against Celtic. After 90 minutes of hacking, punching and spitting, Atlético finished the game with eight men, five of whom were already booked. The 0-0 draw in this first leg at Parkhead helped them on their way to a 2-0 aggregate win, as Los Colchoneros put the 'mad' in Madrid.

There was a far more sedate affair south of the border four years earlier, as the FA toyed with the idea of a third-place play-off game in the FA Cup. In one of the FA's more pointless exercises Manchester United defeated Watford at Highbury in front of a meagre crowd of 15,105. Needless to say, the idea didn't catch on.

APRIL 11

Paving the way for media-friendly England captains with pop star wives everywhere, Billy Wright became the first player to notch up 100 caps for the national side today in 1959 when England defeated Scotland 1-0. Wright captained his country 90 times and led the Three Lions in three successive World Cups in the 1950s. One of those never-booked-or-sent-off types, Wright spent his whole career at Wolves, winning the First Division three times and hitting the headlines for having the first ever football–showbiz marriage when he stepped out with Joy Beverley of the Beverley Sisters.

South African football was in mourning today in 2001 as 43 fans lost their lives in a stampede at Kaiser Chiefs' match with Orlando Pirates at Ellis Park in Johannesburg. A reported 120,000 fans were admitted into the 60,000-seat stadium in what was South Africa's worst ever sporting accident.

APRIL 12

Ask most people who won the first World Cup and they will tell you Uruguay. However, ask people in County Durham and they will tell you something different entirely. The fact that most of the rest of the world has never heard of West Auckland FC does not stop its fans claiming the team are the real winners of the first World Cup, as the provincial side won the first ever Sir Tomas Lipton Trophy today in 1909. The small north-eastern club, made up of miners and traders, was invited to take part in the prestigious international tournament in Italy, and ended up thrashing Juventus 6-1 in the final.

Meanwhile, down in London in 1924, Wembley was hosting its first England game, with Scotland providing the opposition. Billy Walker was the first England player to bag a goal at the original stadium as the two rivals played out a 1-1 draw in front of a disappointing crowd of 37,250.

APRIL 13

Try to imagine that you are a 14th-century peasant. Given that your life consists mainly of simply being downtrodden by virtually everyone, one of your only pleasures in life is a quick game of football on your only day off from the never-ending drudgery that is your work. Well, now you can't even do that because it was today in 1314 that King Edward II issued a proclamation banning football in England.

Manchester United fans probably wished that the game was still banned in 1996, when their visit to the Dell ended in farce. Losing 3-0 to Southampton at half-time, Fergie blamed the poor performance on their grey away kit as the United players were struggling to see each other. Must have been all that grey grass. United came out for the second half in a blue and white number, but even these new digs couldn't prevent a 3-1 loss, and Sir Alex's place in history with the worst excuse of all time.

APRIL 14

Today in 1999 football fans across the country were remarking on two things. The first was Ryan Giggs' wonder-goal that settled their titanic FA Cup semi-final clash with Arsenal and the second was the chest rug that he showed off to the world during his resulting celebration. Giggs' extra-time moment of genius, where he slalomed past a shell-shocked Arsenal side and blasted past David Seaman, set United on the way to their historic treble and was voted their number one goal of all time in a poll.

Giggs' goal had more than a touch of samba magic, which was fitting as it fell on the birthday of Brazil's most famous club, Santos, who were formed today in 1912. The club that is synonymous with Pelé is nicknamed 'The Fish' and became the first team in world football to pass 10,000 goals in 1998.

APRIL 15

In 1989, 96 fans lost their lives and 170 were injured at an FA Cup semi-final between Liverpool and Nottingham Forest at Hillsborough, in what was the greatest loss of life at a British football match ever. The effects of that dark day in Sheffield shocked football to its core and brought about some of the most radical changes in the game's history.

Back in 1967 Scotland came down south to take on the freshly-crowned world champions England where, strictly speaking, only the Home Championship title was on offer. Following Scotland's 3-2 win however, they laid claim to being the 'unofficial World Champions,' as it was England's first defeat since the World Cup. This has since led to the creation of an Unofficial Football World Championship that has seen the likes of Netherlands Antilles and Angola lay claim to being the best in the world.

APRIL 16

Under Brian Clough Nottingham Forest won pretty much everything going and in 1988 the club added another pot to their collection when they won a one-off competition: the Football League Centenary Tournament. The tournament kicked off today at Wembley with 16 clubs turning up to take part in the celebrations for the league's 100th birthday. Clough himself showed what he thought of the whole exercise by not even bothering to attend the contest. Still, it was another thing to stick in the trophy cabinet when Forest beat Sheffield Wednesday in the final.

Liverpool got a manager today in 1992 that, by the end of his spell, many fans hoped would not turn up, as Graeme Souness left his post at Rangers to return to the club where he excelled as a player. He could not reproduce his playing form in the dug out and turned Liverpool from perennial title contenders to also-rans.

APRIL 17

Everyone enjoys an outfield player having to step up as an emergency goalkeeper, and today in 1996 Lucas Radebe of Leeds United had a heck of a job on his hands when he had to go between the sticks at Old Trafford. The South African managed to keep the ball out of the net for almost an hour, but then Roy Keane scored a crucial winner. After the game Sir Alex Ferguson suggested that teams like Leeds tried harder against United, getting a slight reaction from title-chasing boss Kevin Keegan...

Now it's down to 'the Manchester United of the south' as their owner once envisioned. He was partial to the odd conspiracy theory or two, but today in 2003 Mohamed Al-Fayed made one of his wiser decisions, appointing Chris Coleman as Fulham manager. The 32-year-old Welshman would lead the club to safety that season and despite Al-Fayed losing interest in his plaything and spending next to nothing on new players, he would keep them in the top flight until he was given the boot in 2007.

APRIL 18

Before Wembley Stadium was built, the FA Cup final led a nomadic existence, and turned up at Crystal Palace today in 1903 when Bury met Derby County. Thanks to goals from George Ross, Charles Sagar, William Wood, John Plant and a Joe Leeming brace, the Shakers romped home 6-0, which remains the most one-sided final to date.

A metaphorical bomb went off in football on this day in 2021 when a glut of Europe's top clubs announced they had formed a new European Super League, designed to replace UEFA's Champions League. Real Madrid, Juventus, Manchester United and Arsenal were among the clubs who signed up to the new competition – with the founding members guaranteed participation every season – but the backlash was swift and brutal from all quarters. Within days clubs began pulling out until the whole idea was scrapped, for the moment...

APRIL 19

Despite having survived the Soviet invasion, the Taliban regime and subsequent liberation, the Afghanistan football team was disbanded today in 2004 when nine players absconded during a tour of Italy. Having plied their trade in a country where pre-match entertainment used to be preceded by public executions or amputations, the group of players fled to Germany in a bid for asylum.

England's one-time top goalscorer was off the mark today in 1958, as Bobby Charlton made his debut for the Three Lions, smashing home a volley from a Tom Finney cross in a 4-0 win over Scotland at Hampden Park. Charlton wasted no time in adding to his tally, bagging two more in his next game, a 2-1 win over Portugal at Wembley.

APRIL 20

When Fabio Capello was given the England job he claimed that it had always fascinated him. Perhaps this was because today in 1999 the Italian met with FA technical director Howard Wilkinson to discuss taking the hardest job in international football as Kevin Keegan dithered over whether to ditch Fulham and Al-Fayed's millions. Eventually Keegan decided to take on the job, but like the Mounties, it seems the FA always get their man and they appointed Capello in 2007.

One of Keegan's key charges in his England squad was celebrating today in 2001, when Teddy Sheringham was voted Football Writers' Association Player of the Year. The 35-year-old finished the season as Manchester United's top scorer and was the first English player to win the award since his Three Lions 'SAS' strike-force partner Alan Shearer bagged the gong in 1994.

APRIL 21

Somewhere on the Old Trafford pitch there's probably still a bit of Alf-Inge Haaland's knee lying dormant from Roy Keane's infamous crunching tackle that happened today in 2001 in the Manchester derby. Keane freely admitted in his 2002 autobiography that he intended to hurt the Norwegian and get revenge for him implying Keane was faking when he went down with a cruciate ligament injury when Haaland was at Leeds United in 1997.

This unsavoury incident came two years to the day after one of Keane's greatest ever games for Manchester United, when he put in a virtuoso performance in their 3-2 win against Juventus at the Stadio Delle Alpi to book United's place in the final of the European Cup for the first time since 1968. There is a common theme though – Keane was booked early on in the game, meaning that he missed the final.

APRIL 22

He was one of the old school; a perma-tanned, sheepskin-jacketed relic of the dugout, and today in 2004 Ron Atkinson proved that his views were also stuck in the past as he had to abandon his many media commitments following his racist comments over Chelsea's Marcel Desailly. Chelsea had just lost 3-1 to Monaco in a Champions League semi-final first round clash and Big Ron began to rant about the French defender's contribution, not realising he was still live on air to several countries in the Middle East.

'Big Ron' was replaced as Manchester United manager by Alex Ferguson, which ended up being one of the best calls ever by a club board. When Sir Alex retired in 2013, United poached David Moyes from Everton as their new boss, but after a shaky start things only got worse and today in 2014 he was sacked, just nine months after taking the job.

APRIL 23

With it being St George's Day, it would surely be apt to tell you a tale of a triumphant English performance, but instead today is the day that the FA Cup was taken out of the country for the first – and so far only – time, as Cardiff beat Arsenal 1-0 in the 1927 FA Cup final. Cardiff fielded a side featuring the youngest ever player to appear in a final and their keeper Tom Farquarson was rumoured to be an IRA member who always carried a gun with him.

Whilst Cardiff were unable to add to their solitary FA Cup win in the 2008 final, their opponents that day, Portsmouth, also had something to celebrate today in 1949 when they won their first ever league title when they beat Bolton 2-1 at Burnden Park, thereby capping their Golden Jubilee season nicely.

APRIL 24

It was a family affair in Estonia today when Iceland visited Tallinn for a friendly, as former Chelsea striker Eiður Guðjohnsen replaced his dad Arnór when he came on as a second-half substitute. They are the only father and son to have ever played for their country during the same game, and helped Iceland to a 3-2 win. With husband and son on the football field we can only assume mum had gone to Iceland.

On that same day Graeme Souness was doing what he does best and upsetting people. The then Galatasaray manager ran on to the field after a highly-charged Istanbul derby against Fenerbahçe in the Turkish Cup final, planting a Galatasaray flag in the centre circle. The Scot was then given the nickname of 'Ulubatli Souness', after the Turkish martyr Ulubatli Hasan, who made his name in the Siege of Constantinople in 1453.

APRIL 25

To quote Jeff Stelling, they were dancing on the streets of TNS tonight in 2006, when the provincial Welsh side formerly known as Total Network Solutions, and before that Llansantffraid FC, put their naming rights up for auction on eBay. TNS were the first club in the UK to be renamed entirely after their sponsor but unfortunately no one fancied becoming the new subject of Stelling's best joke. The club eventually settled on The New Saints FC when the bids failed to roll in.

Another famous name bowing out today in 2001 was Peter Schmeichel, who retired from international football after playing his 129th game for Denmark. During his 15-year spell between the posts for his national team he was a key member of the victorious Euro 92 squad and captained them 30 times. The sigh of relief from much told-off Danish defenders was heard around Europe.

APRIL 26

Manchester United were born today in 1902 when Newton Heath rebranded themselves following a financial crisis that almost saw the club go under. United's entire existence can be traced back to a St Bernard dog that caught the eye of local industrialist J H Davis. The said mutt was the pride and joy of Heath captain Harry Stafford, who was showing it off on a fundraising event and convinced Davis not only to buy the pet off him but also the club.

Long-serving Coventry City goalkeeper Steve Ogrizovic hung up his gloves today in 2000 after making over 500 appearances for City. His well-earned retirement was interrupted in 2003 when rumours circulated that he had been kidnapped in Kazakhstan, but the panic was averted when the *Coventry Evening Telegraph* tracked him down in his home in Ryton-on-Dunsmore.

APRIL 27

He would have loved it if they'd beaten them, *loved it*. Yes, this day in 1996 witnessed surely the best moment Sky Sports ever broadcast when Kevin Keegan went bonkers live on TV after his Newcastle team had just beaten Leeds. 'He's got to go to Middlesbrough and get something, and... and I tell you honestly, I will love it if we beat them – *love it*,' went the outburst that has gone down in football mind-game history, as Sir Alex Ferguson watched his Manchester United side pull back a 12-point deficit to pip an imploding Toon to the title that season.

As title-fever hit Old Trafford that year, today also marks the birth of the man that designed the stadium, Archibald Leitch, who was born today in 1865. Leitch was responsible for building some of Britain's most aesthetically pleasing and atmospheric stadia, such as Anfield, Ibrox, Highbury and Goodison Park.

APRIL 28

Wembley hosted its first ever football match today in 1923 in what has gone down as the 'White Horse Final' thanks to the efforts of English football's second most famous animal, Billie the grey police horse. Over 300,000 fans turned up for Bolton's clash with West Ham, covering every blade of grass on the pitch, so police called in the horses with Billie taking the lead and clearing the pitch so the match could get under way. Bolton became the first side to climb the 39 steps, winning 2-0 and picking up the first trophy in their history.

There was another first further north, as Leeds United won their first ever league championship when they held rivals Liverpool to a 0-0 draw at Anfield. The point was enough for Don Revie's men to secure the title and they were even loudly hailed by the 27,000 Kopites who chanted 'champions' at their visitors for 20 minutes, a new experience for the usually hated 'dirty' Leeds side.

APRIL 29

In the playground or the park, with jumpers for goalposts, everyone wants to the number 9 when they have a kick about. If not for the events of today in 1933 then there wouldn't be any numbers at all, as Everton and Manchester City's FA Cup final was the first game to feature shirt numbers. This was due to the game's growth as a spectator sport and Everton featured the numbers 1-11 and City made do with 12-22. The Toffeemen won 3-0 thanks to a Dixie Dean brace.

There was another Wembley first in 1970 as Chelsea and Leeds contested the first ever FA Cup final replay. The first clash was a 2-2 draw, so the two rivals met again at Old Trafford, with the southerners coming out 2-1 winners after extra time thanks to goals from Peter Osgood and David Webb.

APRIL 30

Football, as we all know, is a fickle game. One moment you can be on top of the world, the next down and out. Today in 1974 it was the turn of Sir Alf Ramsey to hit rock bottom, as the FA sacked the man who had brought the World Cup home. Six months earlier Sir Alf had overseen England's flop qualification campaign for the 1974 World Cup and despite his success in 1966, Sir Alf had his enemies in the FA who jumped at the opportunity to show him the door.

There were more emotional farewells in Middlesbrough in 1995 as they played their final league match at Ayresome Park. The Smoggies had played there for 92 years and signed off in style as they beat Luton 2-1 to secure the Division One title which meant that the new Riverside Stadium would play host to Premier League football.

FOOTBALL
On This Day

MAY

MAY 1

On this day in 1904 the first international football match between two nations outside of Britain was played when Belgium took on France at Uccle near Brussels. The match ended in a 3-3 draw.

Kevin Keegan once said: 'The only thing I fear is missing an open goal in front of the Kop. I would die if that were to happen. When they start singing "You'll Never Walk Alone" my eyes start to water. There have been times when I've actually been crying while I've been playing.' Today in 1994 the last match was played at Anfield before the Kop was demolished and rebuilt as an all-seater stand. Sadly for the thousands of Liverpool fans packed into it the last player to score in front of the most famous stand in football was Norwich City's Jeremy Goss as the visitors won 1-0.

MAY 2

Sir Stanley Matthews had such an impact on the FA Cup final of 1953 that the match is universally known as 'the Matthews Final'. On this day in 1953 Matthews' Blackpool side were 3-1 down with just 20 minutes left but Stan Mortensen completed his hat-trick to level the score at 3-3 with just a minute remaining. Matthews wasn't finished though and in injury time he burst into the Bolton penalty area and pulled the ball back for Bill Perry to score and give Sir Stanley the only major trophy of his career in an incredible finale.

Today in 1993 Manchester United finally ended their 26-year wait for the league title when their nearest challengers Aston Villa were beaten 1-0 at Villa Park. Also on this day in 2016 an altogether more unlikely championship run was complete when 5,000-1 shots Leicester City won the Premier League. The Foxes went from just avoiding relegation to champions of England in just 12 months – a fairy-tale story for the players and manager Claudio Ranieri. 'I can't think of anything that surpasses it in sporting history,' said celebrity Leicester fan Gary Lineker.

MAY 3

Despite early setbacks including breaking his ankle and fainting while on trial at Metz, Michel Platini finally made his first team debut on this day in 1973 for Nancy against Nîmes Olympique. The following season he established himself in the side and scored 17 goals as the club was promoted to Ligue 1. His finest hour came in the 1984 European Championship when he captained France to victory on home soil, scoring nine goals in just five games and winning the Player of the Tournament award.

From the moment Erling Haaland netted twice on his Premier League debut it became clear he was simply a goalscoring machine. Today in 2023 the Ivan Drago of football scored against West Ham in a 3-0 win for Manchester City. It was his 35th goal of the season, and meant he broke the record for the number of goals scored in a Premier League campaign, previously held by Alan Shearer and Andrew Cole with 34.

MAY 4

Today in 1949 Italy suffered its worst ever sporting disaster when a plane carrying the all-conquering Torino team crashed, wiping out perhaps the greatest ever Italian club side. Nicknamed *Il Grande Torino*, the team had won a record five consecutive league titles between 1943 and 1949 (with two seasons cancelled due to World War II), when their plane crashed on the way back from a friendly with Benfica. The whole country went into mourning and Torino have never hit those heady heights since. Every year on this day a special Mass is held at the crash site and is attended by the current Torino players and families of the victims.

Any loss of life puts football's other problems into stark contrast but that will not have comforted the fans of Leeds United when on this day in 2007 the troubled Yorkshire club went into administration. The drastic action came after the club's relegation to League One was confirmed – the first time the club had been below the top two divisions in English football.

MAY 5

Perhaps the most legendary incident in an FA Cup final occurred today in 1956 when Bert Trautmann, playing in goal for Manchester City, broke his neck with 17 minutes of the match remaining. With no substitutes allowed, Bert was revived with smelling salts and played on, pulling off some crucial saves to help his team to a 3-1 win over Birmingham City. Trautmann had an X-ray four days after the match. 'You should be dead,' Professor David Lloyd Griffiths, an orthopaedic surgeon at Manchester's Royal Infirmary, told him.

Don Revie was a teammate of Trautmann in that final but in 1973 Revie had swapped the pitch for the dugout and on this day that year he saw his all-conquering Leeds team lose the FA Cup final to Second Division Sunderland. Ian Porterfield scored for Sunderland on 31 minutes to give them a 1-0 victory but on the final whistle manager Bob Stokoe ran across the pitch to embrace his goalkeeper Jimmy Montgomery who had made a series of saves to deny Leeds time and again as they pushed for a goal.

MAY 6

On this day in 1972 Leeds won the FA Cup in what was the centenary final of the competition, and the 44th to be played at Wembley. Don Revie's team contained the likes of Billy Bremner, Peter Lorimer and Eddie Gray while opponents Arsenal had Frank McLintock, Alan Ball and George Graham in their ranks. A single goal from Allan Clarke was enough to win the trophy for the Yorkshire team.

From trophy-winning highs to relegation lows for Blackburn Rovers on this day in 1999 when they were relegated to the second tier just four years after being crowned Premier League champions.

FAIRY TALES DO HAPPEN. JIMMY GLASS SCORES HIS FAMOUS LAST-MINUTE GOAL TO PRESERVE CARLISLE UNITED'S LEAGUE STATUS IN MAY 1999 (SEE OVER).

MAY 7

England winning the World Cup in 1966 largely overshadowed any other football achievements that year but on this day Everton defeated Sheffield Wednesday to lift the FA Cup. Managed by former Wednesday boss Harry Catterick, Everton came into the game as the first team to reach the final without conceding a goal. This form immediately went out the window and they were 2-0 down with half an hour left. Two goals from Mike Trebilcock and one from Derek Temple completed the comeback for the Toffees.

Today in 2000, former Everton player and boss Joe Royle was celebrating after leading Manchester City back to the Premiership, having secured promotion with a 4-1 win at Blackburn. Unfortunately for Joe and the Maine Road fans the club was relegated again exactly one year to the day afterwards, thanks to a 2-1 loss at Ipswich.

MAY 8

This day in 1999 saw a Hollywood end to the season for a club fighting for their league survival. Needing a win to avoid relegation to the Conference, Carlisle United were drawing 1-1 with Plymouth five minutes into injury time when on-loan goalkeeper Jimmy Glass came up for a corner. Glass scored to save the club and send Brunton Park wild. Commentator Derek Lacey exclaimed: 'Jimmy Glass! Jimmy Glass! Jimmy Glass, the goalkeeper, has scored a goal for Carlisle United! There's a pitch invasion! There is a pitch invasion! The referee has been swamped – they're bouncing on the crossbar!'

It was truly the end of an era today in 2013 when Sir Alex Ferguson announced he was to retire as manager of Manchester United at the end of the season. The Scot, 71 at the time, won 38 trophies during his 26-year reign at Old Trafford including 13 league titles, two Champions League crowns, five FA Cups and four League Cups. 'It is the right time,' he said. The club are yet to win the Premier League title since Ferguson stood down.

MAY 9

Today in 1936, Bernard Joy, the last amateur player to turn out for the full England side, lined up for the Three Lions in Brussels when they took on Belgium. It was Joy's only cap and he could not prevent England losing 3-2.

A distinct lack of professionalism was on display today in 1973 when Sunderland took on QPR. The Mackems were displaying the FA Cup which they had won just days before. Hoops midfielder Stan Bowles said: 'There were a couple of us who had a bet on who could knock it off the table with the ball first. With the ball at my feet I tear off straight across the park. Everyone on the pitch is just staring at me – and then, bang! The FA Cup goes shooting up in the air. The whole ground knew that I'd done it on purpose – then the Sunderland fans go ape. They want my balls in their sandwiches. At least I got my tenner, and my picture on *News at Ten*. And all because I was just having a bit of a laugh.'

MAY 10

Today in 1986 Liverpool capped a memorable season by beating their cross-town rivals Everton 3-1 in the FA Cup final – seven days after pipping them to the league title. The 1986 cup final was the first to be contested by the two Merseyside teams. Alan Hansen said: 'I'd played in four European Cup finals before that but I can't recall ever being more nervous. It was the Merseyside derby; we were going for the double. I was always pessimistic and the thought of getting beaten in the cup final, it made me unbelievably nervous.'

A year later a young Italian forward named Roberto Baggio scored his first league goal for Fiorentina against Napoli on this day in 1987. The match is better remembered for a Diego Maradona inspired Napoli winning the Scudetto for the first time in their history.

MAY 11

Piano and wig enthusiast Elton John also counts football as one of his interests. A boyhood Watford fan, Elton's family had football heritage – his uncle Roy Dwight played for Nottingham Forest in their 1959 FA Cup final win. On this day in 1976 Elton became chairman of Watford and his spell in charge saw the club experience their most successful period with Graham Taylor as manager.

Bradford City were another club on the up when disaster struck today in 1985. Their game against Lincoln in front of 11,000 fans was supposed to be a celebration of the fact they had just won the Third Division title. However, the day turned to tragedy when a fire quickly engulfed the main stand at Valley Parade. Hundreds were injured and 56 people lost their lives.

Today in 2013 Wigan Athletic had their day of days when they beat favourites Manchester City to win the FA Cup for the first time in their history, thanks to a 91st-minute header from Ben Watson.

MAY 12

On this day in 1979 Manchester United and Arsenal played out the FA Cup final with the most dramatic finish ever. Arsenal were up 2-0 through Talbot and Stapleton in a drab game that came to life on 85 minutes when Gordon McQueen scored for United. Sammy McIlroy added another three minutes later. Any United celebrations were short-lived however, as Alan Sunderland scored with just a minute remaining to win the so-called 'Five-minute Final'.

Today in 1993 Manchester United manager Sir Alex Ferguson had to let go one of his young players that he didn't think would make the grade. Robbie Savage, just 19 at the time, was told he was out and left the club in a daze – so much so that he crashed his car. 'The next thing I know I had crashed and was in hospital: broken bones, cut head, no feeling in my arm, the lot.'

MAY 13

Ajax's decision not to offer Johan Cruyff a new contract at the end of the 1982/83 season would backfire on them spectacularly as the three-time Ballon d'Or winner was so incensed at the snub, he joined arch-rivals Feyenoord and led them to the double, including their first league title for a decade. The Dutch master played his last match on this day in 1984, a 2-1 win over PEC Zwolle.

Today in 2012 saw one of the most dramatic finales to a title race in football history. Manchester United beat Sunderland 1-0 in their final game and thought the Premier League title was theirs as rivals Manchester City were trailing 2-1 to QPR heading into injury time. But Edin Dzeko scored for City with 92 minutes on the clock and then Sergio Aguero sent City fans into dreamland with his 94th-minute winner, immortalised by commentator Martin Tyler's cry of 'AguerOOOOO!!' It sealed City's first title win since 1968.

MAY 14

Wimbledon had only won promotion to the Football League in 1977 but by 1986 they had landed in the top flight, where their physical approach and long-ball tactics proved effective if not popular. Today in 1988 they reached the peak of their achievements when they defeated highly fancied Liverpool in the FA Cup final. A goal from Lawrie Sanchez and a penalty save by Dave Beasant from John Aldridge (the first spot kick ever saved in a final) was enough for the Crazy Gang to lift the trophy in one of the biggest upsets of all time. Exactly 12 years to the day later, they were relegated from the Premier League.

Stoke City reached the FA Cup final for the first time ever on this day in 2011, but lost 1-0 to Manchester City. It was City's first major trophy for 35 years – and the first they had won since the Abu Dhabi Group's takeover three years earlier.

MAY 15

England went continental today in 1963 when Tottenham Hotspur became the first British club to win a major European trophy. They defeated favourites Atletico Madrid 5-1 in the European Cup Winners' Cup final thanks to two goals each from Jimmy Greaves and Terry Dyson and one from John White. Spurs were at the beginning of their heyday under Bill Nicholson and they would go on to pick up trophies galore over the following ten years.

European glory for arguably the world's biggest club today in 2002 when Real Madrid won the European Cup for a record ninth time thanks to a stunning volleyed goal from the most expensive player in the world: Zinedine Zidane. Raul had scored for Real after just eight minutes but Lucio equalised for Bayer Leverkusen five minutes later. Just before half-time Roberto Carlos crossed the ball and Zidane volleyed it straight into the net with his left foot. Great player, great occasion, great goal.

MAY 16

Arsene Wenger's French revolution at Arsenal began to pay dividends today in 1998 when the Gunners defeated Newcastle at Wembley in the FA Cup final thanks to goals from Marc Overmars and Nicolas Anelka. The win meant the club had secured their second league and cup double after Wenger became the first foreign manager to win the league in just his second season at Highbury.

Liverpool fancied a French revolution of their own and in 1998 they brought in Gérard Houllier as manager. On this day in 2001 the Anfield club completed a unique treble when they beat Spanish side Alaves 5-4 in a thrilling UEFA Cup final. Earlier in the season they had beaten Birmingham City to win the League Cup, and had snatched victory from the jaws of defeat in the FA Cup final against Arsenal just four days earlier when Michael Owen scored twice late on after the Gunners had dominated the game.

MAY 17

In 1990 Sir Alex Ferguson's reign at Manchester United was looking under threat. In four years at the club he had won nothing and the fans were beginning to lose patience. Today in 1990 Sir Alex silenced his doubters when he won his first trophy as United boss, beating Crystal Palace in the FA Cup final. The tie needed a replay to find a winner because the first game had ended 3-3 after extra time. The replay was less exciting with a single goal from Lee Martin enough to win Fergie's first trophy and probably save his job.

On this day in 1997 Ruud Gullit became the first foreign manager to win the FA Cup when his Chelsea team beat Middlesbrough, who were playing in their first ever final. Goals from Roberto Di Matteo and Eddie Newton sealed Chelsea's first FA Cup for 27 years.

MAY 18

Real Madrid asserted their dominance of European football early on and won the first five European Cups but undoubtedly the best final of those early years was held on this day in 1960 when the Spanish giants swatted Eintracht Frankfurt aside 7-3 at Hampden Park in Glasgow. In a match some consider to be the greatest ever club game the two original Galácticos, Ferenc Puskás and Alfredo Di Stéfano, had their own personal scoring contest with Puskás coming out on top 4-3, although his second was a penalty.

Perhaps the only match to rival the 1960 game was the 1994 European Cup final which took place on this day, when Fabio Capello's AC Milan team produced one of the best displays of all time to thrash Barcelona 4-0. Barça boss Johan Cruyff had Romario and Hristo Stoichkov in his team but they were overshadowed by Dejan Savićević, who made one and scored one in an outstanding display. Daniele Massaro got two and Marcel Desailly completed the scoring for the Rossoneri.

MAY 19

England's World Cup winning captain Bobby Moore was also captain of West Ham and played for the Irons for 15 years. Under manager Ron Greenwood the club won the FA Cup in 1964 and on this day in 1965 Moore captained the team to victory in the European Cup Winners' Cup final at Wembley. Two goals from Alan Sealey was enough to see off 1860 Munich.

Matthew Le Tissier was as inspirational for Southampton as Moore had been for West Ham and on this day in 2001 the man nicknamed 'Le God' had the last word in the last competitive match at the Dell before the Saints moved to their new home, the St Mary's Stadium. Arsenal were the opposition and the game looked like ending in a 2-2 draw before Le Tissier came on late on with the fans hoping for one more moment of magic from their hero. He did not disappoint and with just two minutes remaining he scored with a trademark beautifully struck volley to send the Dell crowd wild. They invaded the pitch to mob Le Tissier and the rest of the team.

MAY 20

In 1995 neither Everton nor Manchester United had had good seasons by their standards. Double winners the previous season, United had lost the Premiership to Blackburn while Everton had only just avoided relegation. The two teams met in the FA Cup final on this day with the Red Devils expected to claim the trophy. Without the suspended Cantona, the injured Kanchelskis and the cup-tied Andy Cole, United struggled and Joe Royle's Everton won thanks to a Paul Rideout goal.

Cup specialists Chelsea were at it again today in 2000 when they won the last FA Cup final to be held at Wembley before the stadium was rebuilt. In goal for Aston Villa was David James, who fumbled a Gianfranco Zola free kick into the path of Roberto Di Matteo, who scored the only goal of the game.

MAY 21

FIFA was born on this day in 1904. The Fédération Internationale de Football Association was formed in Paris with Belgium, Denmark, France, the Netherlands, Spain, Sweden and Switzerland the founder members. FIFA now has more than 200 member nations, which is more than the United Nations.

Apart from overseeing the laws of the game, FIFA's main job is to organise the World Cup. One of the traditions of participating countries in each tournament is the usually terrible World Cup anthem. Perhaps England's best offering, New Order's 'World in Motion', was released today in 1990. A few of the England squad feature in the song with Gazza on backing vocals but John Barnes stole the show with his famous Barnsey rap: 'Catch me if you can/ Cos I'm the England man/And what you're looking at/Is the master plan.' Word, Barnesy.

MAY 22

AC Milan achieved the first of their European Cup triumphs on this day in 1963 at Wembley, beating Benfica 2-1. The Portuguese side had taken the lead through Eusébio in the 18th minute but two goals from José Altafini in the second half won the cup for the Italian giants.

Despite nine appearances in the European Cup final Juventus have not fared as well as Milan, losing all but two of them. Their first victory was in 1985 against Liverpool, although the win was overshadowed by the Heysel disaster. Their second win came on this day in 1996 when they faced Ajax in a rematch of the 1973 final when Johan Cruyff had inspired the Dutch side to a 1-0 win. This time around it was Juve's turn to triumph although they needed a penalty shoot-out to do it after Fabrizio Ravanelli's opener was cancelled out by a Jari Litmanen equaliser.

May 23

When England lost 6-3 to the Mighty Magyars of Hungary at Wembley 1953 it was a humbling experience that put an end to England's unshakeable belief in their own superiority. Eager to reclaim some credibility after the thrashing by Ferenc Puskas and his team, England agreed to a rematch in Hungary the following year as a warm-up for the World Cup in Switzerland. Far from exacting revenge, on this day in 1954 in the Népstadion in Budapest England were again taught a lesson in football by the Hungarians; they thrashed them 7-1. It remains England's heaviest ever defeat.

Perhaps England fans were fearing a humiliating repeat of those Hungary games today in 1989 when the lowest crowd ever turned up for an England home match. Just 15,628 spectators filed into an eerily empty Wembley Stadium for the 0-0 draw with Chile. The Tube strike in London that night probably didn't help matters.

May 24

On this day in 1984 Terry Venables got his 'El Tel' moniker when he was appointed manager of Barcelona. He steered the club to their first league title in 11 years. In 1986 he signed Gary Lineker and Mark Hughes but could only manage second place in La Liga and lost on penalties to Steaua Bucharest in the European Cup final. The sack soon followed.

Another manager was having trouble with his star player today in 2002 when Roy Keane flew home from the Irish training camp just days before the World Cup began. Keane was unhappy with the squad's preparations for the finals and vented his frustrations at manager Mick McCarthy who eventually had to send him home. Keane is reported to have said: 'I don't rate you as a manager and I don't rate you as a person. The only reason I have any dealings with you is that somehow you are the manager of my country and you're not even Irish!'

MAY 25

By the twelfth year of the European Cup, the competition had been won each year by either Real Madrid, Benfica, Internazionale or AC Milan. On this day in 1967 Jock Stein's Celtic travelled to Lisbon to take on the mighty Inter. Stein's team, famously made up of players all born within a 30-mile radius of Celtic Park, were rank outsiders against the Italians who had won in '64 and '65. Roared on by 12,000 Celtic fans, the 'Lisbon Lions' beat Inter to win the cup and shock the world.

The world was perhaps more shocked today in 1970 when England captain Bobby Moore was arrested in Colombia, accused of stealing a bracelet from a jewellers. England were preparing for their World Cup defence in Mexico when Moore had his collar felt, but when it emerged that the tracksuit he had been wearing while in the shop had no pockets, he was released without charge and went on to play in England's epic clash with Brazil.

MAY 26

Today in 1989 Liverpool and Arsenal played out one of the most thrilling title deciders England has ever seen. Liverpool were at home and didn't even need to win – just avoiding a two-goal defeat would be enough to win it for them, and they were confident having won their last ten home games. Alan Smith gave Arsenal the lead on 52 minutes but with just 80 seconds left the Liverpool fans were celebrating. Michael Thomas had other ideas and he chipped the ball over Bruce Grobbelaar to win the title for Arsenal, and inspire Nick Hornby to write *Fever Pitch*.

Anything Arsenal can do, Manchester United can do better and it was on this day in 1999 that the Red Devils completed an historic treble when two late, late goals from Sheringham and Solskjaer were enough to beat Bayern Munich in the most dramatic finish to a European Cup final ever seen. The Old Trafford club also won the Premiership and FA Cup that season.

MAY 27

Today in 1992 all the clubs in the First Division resigned from the Football League en masse and the FA Premier League was formed. The move made no difference whatsoever to the competition or the rules but it did mean the top flight could now negotiate its own broadcast and sponsorship rights independently of the Football League.

After breaking into the senior Liverpool team in 1997, Michael Owen wasted little time in becoming one of his era's best goalscorers. Today in 1998 the 18-year-old striker scored his first England goal. His strike came in a pre-World Cup friendly with Morocco and he would go on to announce his arrival as a top-class striker to the world in England's group game with Argentina.

MAY 28

During the 1960s and 1970s Don Revie's Leeds United team snarled and scrapped their way to just about every trophy that was on offer. The one exception was the European Cup, and they never came closer than today in 1975, when Leeds, by then under the stewardship of Jimmy Armfield, lost a controversial final to Bayern Munich in Paris. The referee turned down two good penalty appeals for Leeds and disallowed a Peter Lorimer goal for a dubious offside call. Two late Bayern goals won it for the Germans but manager Franz Beckenbauer admitted: 'In the end we were winners but we were very, very lucky.'

Nottingham Forest went one better than Leeds, lifting the European Cup in 1979 to the delight of their fans. Incredibly Brian Clough's team managed to retain their crown the following season and on this day in 1980 John Robertson scored the only goal in the win over a Hamburg team containing Kevin Keegan at the Bernabéu in Madrid.

MAY 29

Ten years earlier his team had been ripped apart in the Munich air disaster but Sir Matt Busby rebuilt and on this day in 1968 crash survivor Bobby Charlton played in the team that won the European Cup, the perfect way to honour the fallen players. Charlton, George Best and Brian Kidd all scored to beat Eusébio's Benfica at Wembley – they became the first English club to win the trophy.

Liverpool have won the European Cup six times but today in 1985 they lost in a final that was completely overshadowed by events off the pitch. As fans of Liverpool and Juventus clashed, a retaining wall in the Heysel stadium collapsed killing 39 people, mostly Italian fans. Juventus won 1-0 thanks to a Michel Platini penalty.

MAY 30

The year before Heysel, Liverpool had won the European Cup thanks in no small part to their eccentric goalkeeper Bruce Grobbelaar. Their final opponents were Roma and the match was played in the Stadio Olimpico – Roma's home ground. The score was level at 1-1 after extra time so penalties were needed. Grobbelaar used his famous spaghetti legs routine to try to put off his opponents and it seemed to work as Bruno Conti and Francesco Graziani both missed their spot kicks. Grobbelaar said: 'People said I was being disrespectful to their players, but I was just testing their concentration under pressure. I guess they failed that test.'

Today in 1996, just before the European Championships started, the England team flew home from a tour of Hong Kong. The trip coincided with Paul Gascoigne's 29th birthday and the players celebrated like it was, well, Gazza's birthday. Cathay Pacific, the airline that brought them home, reported £5,000 worth of damage to the plane that they said was caused by the players who had continued their drunken binge on to the flight.

MAY 31

Would you have the balls to sack Alex Ferguson? No, neither would we, but Willie Todd did on this day in 1978. Todd was chairman of St Mirren and Fergie had been in charge for four years but already the big time was calling in the shape of Aberdeen. Todd later said Ferguson had made it clear he was going to Aberdeen and even wanted to take some players with him, so he sacked him for breach of contract – the only man ever to fire him.

A transfer on this day in 2006 smacked of an owner foisting a player on his manager, like it or not. Roman Abramovich wanted more flair in his Chelsea team, so he bought AC Milan goal machine Andriy Shevchenko for £30m. Despite a strike rate at Milan of more than a goal every other game, Sheva looked a shadow of his former self at Stamford Bridge, scoring just nine league goals in two seasons at the club.

FOOTBALL
On This Day

JUNE

JUNE 1

Paul Gascoigne's England career was over today in 1998, ending as explosively as it began. When Glenn Hoddle told Gazza he hadn't made his World Cup 98 squad the midfielder smashed a lamp and chair in Hoddle's hotel room, injuring his foot in the process. Hoddle's decision was brought on by photos in the tabloid press the week before of Gazza tucking into a kebab in the early hours of the morning.

There was also the dawn of a new era for England in 2007, as the new Wembley Stadium played host to its first England game when the Three Lions took on Brazil. Captain John Terry had the honour of scoring the first ever goal, but, as usual, it was David Beckham that took the limelight, providing the assist as he returned to the national team for the first time since the 2006 World Cup, and Steve McClaren ate a slice of humble pie.

JUNE 2

There was an almighty dust-up today in 1962 as Chile and Italy played out the 'Battle of Santiago' in their World Cup clash. Ninety minutes of horror tackles, dirty tactics and flying fists was best summed up by David Coleman when he introduced the highlights on the BBC: 'Good evening. The game you are about to see is the most stupid, appalling, disgusting and disgraceful exhibition of football, possibly in the history of the game.' But then again Coleman had never had to sit through 90 minutes of Sam Allardyce football.

The game was in the headlines for the wrong reasons again in 1985, as English clubs were banned by UEFA from playing in Europe following the Heysel stadium disaster the week before. The ban eventually lasted for five years – and six for Liverpool – as the authorities attempted to tackle the hooliganism problem that was plaguing English football.

JUNE 3

Striking a chord with B-boys everywhere, Peter Crouch proved he had the moves of a young Travolta today in 2006 when he performed a flawless robot dance after scoring a hat-trick against Jamaica at Old Trafford. Inspired by the Arctic Monkey's call to 'dance like a robot from 1984' in their single 'I Bet That You Look Good on the Dancefloor', Crouchie brought the robo-boogie back from the dead, as drunk fans across the nation were roboting quicker than you could say 'good touch for a big man'.

Here's a tip for anyone planning a wedding anytime soon – if you're planning a romantic summer do and tying the knot on this day, you might want to think again. Over the last 40-odd years England have played more games on this day than any other, with the Crouch-inspired 6-0 romp over Jamaica being the tenth time the Three Lions have been in action today since 1981, so don't blame us if no one turns up…

JUNE 4

England versus the Mighty Ducks may sound like a rubbish sequel to Emilio Estevez's finest hour, but this is what we had in 1988 as England warmed up for the European Championships by taking on Aylesbury United, nicknamed The Ducks. We're not sure whose idea it was to take on the reigning Beazer Homes League Premier Division champions, led by the gloriously named striker Cliff Hercules, but England's 7-0 win did little for their fortunes in West Germany, where they lost all three games.

While he was twiddling his thumbs between the sticks that day Peter Shilton had a chance to reflect on the anniversary of his debut that took place in 1966 when he turned out for Leicester against Everton. During his 31-year career Shilton notched up over 1,000 club games and is England's record caps holder on 125.

JUNE 5

For the neutral, penalty shoot-outs are one of the best things in football. Anything that makes John Terry and Cristiano Ronaldo cry in the space of seconds (see the 2008 Champions League final) is worth its weight in gold. However, the dreaded shoot-out has only been around since 1970, so before then stalemates were all decided by lady luck and the toss of a coin. Today in 1968 a place in the European Championship final was decided with a simple 'heads or tails' as the Soviet Union captain Albert Shesternyov called wrong and Italy progressed.

Later that evening England took on Yugoslavia in the other semi in Florence and yet more history was made. The Yugoslavs set out to frustrate England with constant fouling, hoping that they would lose their heads. Eventually Tottenham's Alan Mullery lashed out and became the first ever England player to be sent off. England lost 1-0 to a late Dragan Džajić goal.

JUNE 6

Spurs believed that their act-first-think-later strategy was going to pay off today in 2004 when they finally got round to replacing Glenn Hoddle, who they had sacked in September 2003. After persisting with caretaker David Pleat for a whole season, during which time bookmakers took bets on over 85 different names for the job at White Hart Lane, Tottenham eventually landed French boss Jacques Santini. Spurs fans believed they had landed their Arsene Wenger, but after only 13 very dull league games that saw Spurs score six goals he was on his bike.

England kicked off their first ever summer tour today in 1908 when they took on Austria in Vienna. The Three Lions' first ever game outside the British Isles ended with an emphatic 6-1 win with Chelsea pair Jimmy Windridge and George Hilsdon both helping themselves to a brace. Those were the days…

JUNE 7

The 1970 World Cup exploded into life today, as World Champions England took on Brazil in a match that had the lot. Gordon Banks' first-half save was described by Pelé as 'like a salmon leaping up a waterfall' and is widely hailed as the best save ever made. Bobby Moore's famous tackle on Jairzinho was good enough to be referenced in Baddiel and Skinner's 'Three Lions', but even he couldn't stop him scoring the only goal of the game. Showing enormous mutual respect, Pelé and Moore embraced at the final whistle, giving us one of football's most iconic images. Football was indeed the winner.

In 2002 England again found themselves facing South American opposition, as they were able to extract revenge for 1986 and 1998 against Argentina. David Beckham had every reason to be smug when he put away a penalty on the stroke of half-time to help consign the Argentinians to a first-round exit.

JUNE 8

Although Pelé's prediction that an African side would win the World Cup before 2000 proved to be wide of the mark, Cameroon showed that they meant business today in 1990 when they stunned reigning world champions Argentina by beating them 1-0. 'They thought they would make a rabbit stew of us,' claimed Cameroon's 38-year-old striker Roger Milla, who inspired the Indomitable Lions to make it all the way to the quarter-finals where they bowed out to England.

The Bronx after dark is not always the best place to be, but this is where England found themselves in 1953 when they kicked off their American tour at the iconic Yankee Stadium. England got their shock 1950 loss to the USA out of their system with a 6-3 win in what was their first match to be played under floodlights.

JUNE 9

Paul Ince became the first black player to captain England during their game with the USA in 1993. Ince was handed the armband for the clash in Foxboro Stadium in Massachusetts in the absence of David Platt and Tony Adams but was unable to prevent a 2-0 loss as England hit a rough patch and failed to make it to the following year's World Cup. Since his retirement as a player Ince has been breaking down more boundaries, becoming the first black Englishman to manage in the Premier League with Blackburn Rovers.

Another England star, Tom Finney, had reason to celebrate today in 1961 as he was awarded the OBE in the Birthday Honours List. Preston's inspirational captain scored over 200 goals in his 500 matches for club and country and had retired a year earlier.

JUNE 10

Jimmy Greaves went all Doctor Dolittle on us today in 1962 when he tackled an unlikely pitch invader during England's World Cup clash with Brazil in Chile. When a stray dog ran on to the pitch he managed to evade capture from officials and players until Greavsie got down on all fours and gave him the come-hither eyes. Showing the reactions that bagged him 39 goals that season, Greavsie grabbed the dog by the neck, bringing cheers from the crowd. These cheers turned to laughter seconds later when the dog urinated all over Greaves' shirt. Garrincha found it particularly funny, enjoying the incident so much he took the dog home with him.

Today in 2023 Manchester City finally sealed the Champions League glory the club had been chasing since becoming one of the biggest players in European football, when they beat Internazionale 1-0 in the final. It capped a treble season for City in which they also won the Premier League and the FA Cup – matching Manchester United's achievement in 1999.

JUNE 11

As the home nations' only representative in the 1978 World Cup, Scotland had a chance to show what they could do in the international arena. Obviously it goes without saying that they went out in the group stage, but they did find time to score one of the great World Cup goals when they took on Holland in their final match. The Scots went in needing to win by three goals and took a 3-1 lead when Archie Gemmill linked up with Kenny Dalglish as he ran into the box to score Mark Renton from *Trainspotting*'s favourite ever goal. However, it's the hope that kills you, and Scotland were coming home when they could only win 3-2.

One Scot was celebrating today though, as Alex Ferguson became Sir Alex Ferguson when he was knighted in the Queen's Birthday Honours list in 1999 following Manchester United's treble-winning season.

JUNE 12

His father wasn't a fan and neither was he. Following Edward II's ban on playing football in cities, Edward III went the whole hog today in 1349 and ditched it everywhere. His reasoning was that the growth of the game was having a detrimental effect on the nation's archery skills, as England was in the midst of the Hundred Years' War against France, so a kick around in the park would have left you in the slammer.

One player that wasn't having any problems with his accuracy today in 2002 was Southampton's Swedish midfielder Anders Svensson, who hit the bullseye with a 30-yard free kick in his country's World Cup clash with Argentina. The 1-1 draw was enough to win the group for Sweden and send favourites Argentina crashing out of the tournament in South Korea and Japan.

JUNE 13

When you're the world's most famous player, you're going to have your run-ins with the press. Whereas some players are happy to see their picture everywhere, others take exception. Today in 1998 Diego Maradona was given a suspended prison sentence for going one further than the old hat-and-glasses disguise as he shot at an assembled group of hacks with an air rifle outside his Buenos Aires home.

England managed to snatch defeat from the claws of victory in their opening European Championship game in 2004, as Zinedine Zidane scored twice in injury time to give Les Bleus a 2-1 victory. A first-half Frank Lampard goal looked to have secured the win for the Three Lions, but Zizou's imperious free kick and penalty ensured that the legions of England fans in the Estádio da Luz in Lisbon had to endure another night of what could have been.

JUNE 14

They've spent most of their existence meandering around the lower regions of English football but today in 2002, Exeter City hit the headlines the world over, as the King of Pop himself, Michael Jackson, visited the club as part of a charity event. Jacko shamoned his way down to Devon courtesy of the club's new chairman, spoon-bending enthusiast Uri Geller, who said he wouldn't use his powers to influence performance on the pitch and he wasn't joking – the club finished bottom of the whole Football League during his only season at the helm.

Jackson spent most of 1987 wondering 'who's bad?' so we'll point him in the direction of Carlos Caszely. The Chilean striker became the first player to be sent off in the World Cup today in 1974 following a foul on West Germany's Berti Vogts.

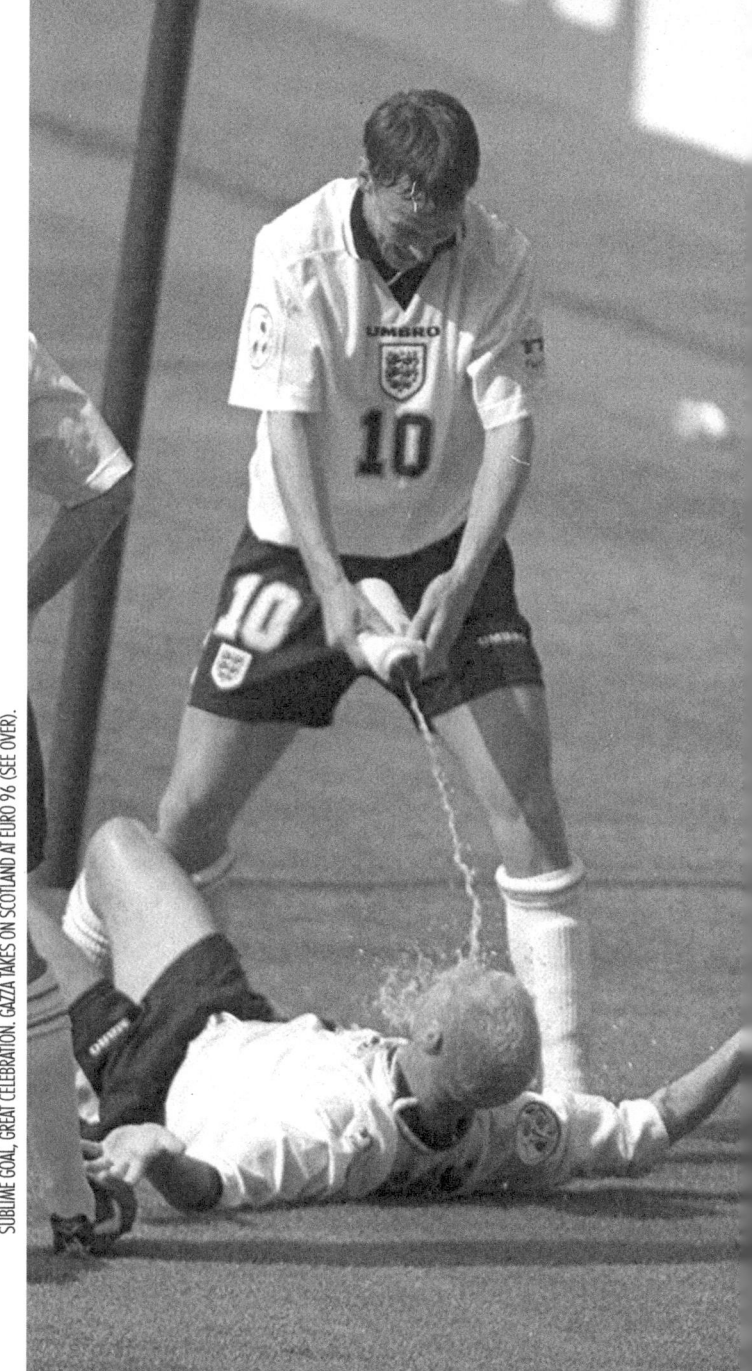

SUBLIME GOAL, GREAT CELEBRATION. GAZZA TAKES ON SCOTLAND AT EURO 96 (SEE OVER).

JUNE 15

England's Euro 96 campaign was up and running today as they took on Scotland for the first time since 1989. The game swung on a second-half Gary McAllister penalty that was saved by David Seaman with the score at 1-0 to England. Minutes later Paul Gascoigne scored what was later voted as the best goal the old Wembley Stadium ever saw as he lifted the ball over Colin Hendry's head and volleyed past his Rangers teammate Andy Goram, celebrating with a recreation of the 'dentist's chair' routine that had been splashed across the papers in the run-up to the tournament.

Back in 1911, England captain Bob Crompton's celebrations at becoming his country's most capped player were slightly more muted, as the Blackburn full-back was presented with a portrait of himself after breaking Steve Bloomer's record of 23 caps.

JUNE 16

Today in 1982 England were competing in their first World Cup since 1970, and Bryan Robson wasted no time in getting their campaign up and running. Captain Marvel scored after just 27 seconds in the opening match against France as England cantered to a 3-1 win. It was the fastest goal ever scored in World Cup history – a record that stood until Hakan Şükür scored after just 10 seconds for Turkey against South Korea in 2002.

England were making heavier weather of their Euro 2016 campaign today, and fell behind to a first-half Gareth Bale strike against Wales. Jamie Vardy equalised ten minutes into the second half before Daniel Sturridge netted a 91st-minute winner. It was England's only win of the tournament as they were beaten 2-1 by Iceland in their first knockout match to end Roy Hodgson's tenure as England boss.

JUNE 17

There was another iconic image of England failure today in 1992, when Gary Lineker's England career ended with the striker to be forever marooned on 48 international goals, one short of Sir Bobby Charlton's record, after his substitution against Sweden in the European Championship. Graham Taylor's gamble backfired and he was lambasted in the press when England lost the do-or-die game. *The Sun* famously ran the headline 'SWEDES 2 TURNIPS 1', putting a picture of Taylor's head on the aforementioned root vegetable.

With the Covid-19 pandemic sweeping the globe in 2020, football in the UK had been suspended in mid-March – initially just for a matter of weeks. In the end the pause in the season lasted until this day. The Premier League resumed with two matches: Aston Villa drew 0-0 at home to Sheffield United, while Manchester City swept Arsenal aside 3-0.

JUNE 18

It's the hope that kills you. Today in 1996 England looked like world-beaters when they took down the much-fancied Dutch team 4-1 in Euro 96. Two goals apiece from the SAS strike force of Shearer and Sheringham gave us one of England's best performances in years and got the whole nation believing football, as Baddiel and Skinner suggested, was indeed coming home. Needless to say, we all know how the tournament would end...

England also beat Scotland at Euro 96, and on this day 25 years later the two sides squared up again at Wembley in the group stages of Euro 2020. This time round there was far less excitement than England's 2-0 win in 1996, as the oldest rivals in international football played out a 0-0 draw.

JUNE 19

Italian dictator Benito Mussolini brought a new motivational trick to his national team who faced Hungary in the World Cup final today in 1938. Seeing the World Cup as an opportunity for a spot of national posturing, *Il Duce* sent the squad a telegram that simply read: 'Vincere o morire'. Literally translated this means 'Win or die' and what do you know? It did the trick as Italy won 4-2. Antal Szabo, the Hungarian goalie, said after the match: 'I may have let in four goals, but at least I saved their lives.'

Welsh football peaked today in 1958 when they took on Brazil in the World Cup quarter-final. Led by the irrepressible John Charles, Wales had seen off the Mighty Magyars of Hungary in the group stage but met their match against Brazil thanks to a goal from 17-year-old Pelé, who became the youngest ever scorer in World Cup history. Wales didn't qualify for another World Cup until 2022.

JUNE 20

A touch of class was added to the Premier League today in 1995 when Boring Boring Arsenal got quite a bit more exciting and signed Dennis Bergkamp from Internazionale for a then record fee of £7.5m. The non-flying Dutchman thrived under the stewardship of Arsene Wenger, who joined him in 1996, winning three Premiership titles and four FA Cups. The stats only tell half the story though, as Bergkamp played some of the most stylish football this country has ever seen.

How the English team could have done with a Bergkamp-type influence today in 2000, when they faced Romania in their final European Championship group game in Charleroi. Instead the Three Lions had Phil Neville, who gave away a last-minute penalty that former Wolves striker Ioan Ganea fired home to give the Romanians a 3-2 win and send England home.

JUNE 21

The so-called 'greatest team ever' were strutting their stuff and winning the World Cup today in 1970, as the Brazil side that featured Pelé, Jairzinho et al hoisted the Jules Rimet trophy for the third time. Their opponents that day were Italy, who kept the Seleção at bay for over an hour, but eventually succumbed 4-1. Carlos Alberto's second-half strike is seen by many as the greatest goal scored in a World Cup final, as he ended a flowing move by leathering it past the hapless Enrico Albertosi and into the history books.

Their successors in the famous yellow shirts were also at it in the 2002 World Cup, knocking out England in the quarter-finals, thanks to Ronaldinho's 40-yard free kick that, not for the first time, caught David Seaman unawares. Ronaldinho was sent off minutes later for a foul on Danny Mills, but England were unable to overcome the 10-man Brazil side.

JUNE 22

Two of football's most famous goals were scored in a five-minute spell today in 1986 as Diego Maradona showed the world both sides of his personality in the World Cup quarter-final in Mexico City. Whereas Maradona claimed his first goal was helped by 'the hand of God', the English press saw it as 'the hand of the Devil' as post-Falklands War relations were a tad gritty. Just to rub it in, Maradona then went and skipped past five England players en route to scoring one of the greatest goals ever seen to knock England out.

There was another memorable World Cup moment today in 1974. Zaire were the first black African nation to qualify for the tournament and were having a bit of a torrid time after losing 2-0 to Scotland and then 9-0 to Yugoslavia. Their final game was against holders Brazil and defender Mwepu Llunga got a bit too over-excited waiting for a Brazilian free-kick, charging out from the wall and booting the ball down the pitch.

JUNE 23

While England fans think their national team holds the British monopoly on glorious and not-so-glorious failure at international tournaments, the Tartan Army have had their fair share of crushing disappointments in far-flung places as well. Today in 1998 Craig Brown's troops were on their way home following a lacklustre 3-0 defeat to Morocco. This was despite the pleas of Del Amitri, whose official anthem for the squad was pessimistically, but ultimately realistically entitled 'Don't Come Home Too Soon'.

One of South America's worst stadium disasters occurred after River Plate and Boca Juniors' match today in 1968. Seventy-four fans were killed and more than 150 injured as the crowd surged towards a closed exit, not realising those at the front were being crushed by the closed passageway.

JUNE 24

Clashes between Holland and Germany rarely pass without incident, so when the two rivals met today during Italia 90 it was no real surprise that Rudi Völler and Frank Rijkaard were sent off for scrapping after only 20 minutes. As the pair walked off the pitch Rijkaard raised the bar and spat on Völler, with the gob hanging off the German's impressive perm for all to see. Nice. The Germans managed to compose themselves, winning 2-1 on the way to their third title.

There was more penalty heartbreak for England on this day at Euro 2012 when Roy Hodgson's side managed to hold an Andrea Pirlo-inspired Italy to a 0-0 draw after extra time in the quarter-finals, but couldn't shake the old penalty shoot-out curse with Ashleys Cole and Young missing to see England knocked out. It meant England's record in tournament shoot-outs stood at one win in seven.

June 25

The most controversial World Cup of the 20th century climaxed today in 1978, as Argentina picked up the trophy in their backyard. A military junta had taken over the country two years earlier and the tournament was beset by political interference – with match-fixing rumoured to have taken place to ensure that the host nation made it to the final, where they beat a Johan Cryuff-less Holland 3-1.

Ten years later Holland beat the Soviet Union 2-0 in the Euro 88 final, with Marco van Basten following up Ruud Gullit's first-half goal by scoring *that* volley to secure the Oranje's first ever major title.

Liverpool ended their 30-year wait for a league title today in 2020 when a Manchester City defeat to Chelsea sealed the championship for Jürgen Klopp's side.

June 26

England went crashing out of Euro 96 today in suitably predictable fashion. With the nation whipped up into a frenzy by over-excited tabloids and a couple of decent performances, the Three Lions took on Germany at Wembley for a place in the final. With the sides locked at 1-1 after extra time it went down to what every England fan dreads – penalties. Somehow Terry Venables' charges managed to score their first five spot kicks, but when Gareth Southgate stepped up his nerve failed him, leaving Andreas Möller to slot home the winner.

It's not all doom and gloom for England today though, as 1990 saw a dramatic win over Belgium thanks to David Platt's goal in the last minute of injury time. The second-half substitute scored a magnificent volley on the turn to send his side into the quarter-final where they would face surprise package Cameroon.

JUNE 27

David O'Leary paid the price for his outspoken and forthright attitude today in 2002 when he was sacked by Leeds United. Despite taking his team of 'babies' to the European Cup semi-finals a year earlier, the wheels were starting to fall off the Elland Road bandwagon when the club failed to qualify for the competition and Peter Ridsdale's 'living the dream' gamble didn't pay off. Throw in his book entitled *Leeds United on Trial*, released when two of his players were in court accused of assault, and the dressing room was well and truly lost.

England have twice been knocked out of major tournaments on this day: firstly by Germany in a humbling 4-1 defeat for the Three Lions at the 2010 World Cup, and secondly in an even more humbling 2-1 loss to Iceland that saw England crash out of Euro 2016.

JUNE 28

Much to the delight of almost everyone in the country, referee Graham Poll was sent home from the 2006 World Cup today following his gaffe in Australia's crucial group match with Croatia. When he gave Croatian Josip Šimunić not one, not two, but three yellow cards before sending him off, the 'Thing from Tring' had to leave Germany with his tail between his legs.

A year later, Chris Coleman jetted out to become Real Sociedad's new manager after being sacked by Fulham in April. This was despite keeping the club in the Premiership during his four year spell in charge. Sociedad were relegated from La Liga last season for the first time in 40 years, finishing 19th out of 20. Cookie was recommended for the job by fellow Welshman and former Sociedad manager John Toshack but after a change in the Basque club's board he would only last six months.

JUNE 29

Long before he became perhaps the game's most famous-ever player, Pelé was a fresh-faced teenager about to dazzle the world. Today in 1958 he heralded his arrival with a match-winning performance in the World Cup final, scoring two goals as a 17-year-old as Brazil won their first ever Jules Rimet trophy.

Eight years earlier England had entered their first ever World Cup, but set the tone for many tournaments to come as they were on the receiving end of one of football's biggest ever upsets. Taking on a USA team that had lost their last seven games by a combined score of 45-2, England's finest went down 1-0 in what is known as the 'Miracle on Grass' stateside as they crashed out of the tournament in the group stage.

JUNE 30

England exited the 1998 World Cup today in typically dramatic fashion when Argentina defeated the Three Lions in Saint-Étienne. A breathless game saw 18-year-old Michael Owen score one of England's best ever goals, David Beckham sent off after Diego Simeone's histrionics, Sol Campbell have a late winner disallowed and then the inevitable shoot-out loss. This time it was the turn of David Batty and Paul Ince to fail from 12 yards, as Argentine keeper Carlos Roa saved from the gritty midfield pair.

Four years later Argentina's greatest rivals Brazil were picking up their fifth World Cup crown after beating Germany 2-0 in the final. Ronaldo scored both goals to win the cup and complete a remarkable footballing resurrection after his limp display in the 1998 final when Brazil lost to France. His two strikes took his tally for the tournament to eight and propelled him to Galáctico status as Real Madrid came-a-calling shortly after.

FOOTBALL
On This Day

JULY

JULY 1

No one saw it coming and it had huge ramifications at the top level of English and European football: today in 2003 Russian billionaire Roman Abramovich paid around £140m to buy Chelsea from Ken Bates. He said: 'I don't want to throw my money away, but it's really about having fun and that means success and trophies.' He then embarked on a spending spree that made Jack Walker look tight-fisted and won the club their first league title in 50 years, ushering in a period of unparalleled success for the club before he was forced to sell up in 2022 following Russia's invasion of Ukraine.

International football took centre stage today in 2012 when Spain crushed Italy 4-0 in the Euro 2012 final in Kyiv. It was the greatest winning margin in the history of European Championship finals, and meant Spain became the first team to win the trophy twice in succession – and the first to win three consecutive major tournaments, *La Roja* having also triumphed in the 2010 World Cup.

JULY 2

Uruguay picked up their second World Cup win at the 1950 tournament in Brazil but today in 1950 they completed an 8-0 rout of South American opponents Bolivia in their only group match after Scotland and Turkey pulled out of the competition. Oscar Míguez scored a hat-trick in the match and is Uruguay's record World Cup goalscorer with eight goals.

The England players came home early to disappointed fans but the worst they had to endure was a bit of a hard time at away grounds. Tragically the same was not so for Colombian defender Andres Escobar. In the 1994 World Cup Escobar had scored an own goal against the USA to effectively eliminate Colombia in the first round. On this day in 1994 Escobar was gunned down in the Colombian city of Medellín, with his own goal the supposed motive.

JULY 3

Less than 24 hours after helping France win Euro 2000 Robert Pires celebrated by signing for Arsenal, that home-away-from-home for Frenchmen in London, on this day. The winger signed for £5.3m from Marseille, with Gunners boss Arsène Wenger the key to the deal according to Pires, who said at the time: 'I would have preferred to have played for Real Madrid, but the words of Wenger gave me more security.' Pires won the league twice and the FA Cup three times in his spell at Highbury.

With the score 1-1 after extra time in England's round of 16 match with Colombia at the 2018 World Cup, Three Lions fans everywhere braced for the inevitable penalty shoot-out defeat. But just minutes later there were wild celebrations when Eric Dier scored the winner after Jordan Pickford saved from Carlos Bacca. It was the first time England had won a penalty shoot-out since Euro 96.

JULY 4

When the 1954 World Cup in Switzerland started the Mighty Magyar Hungarian national side were in their pomp and were pre-tournament favourites. In the group stage an 8-3 win over West Germany only shortened Hungary's odds of becoming world champions. On this day they met West Germany again in the final in the Wankdorf Stadium in Berne. The injured Ferenc Puskás and Zoltán Czibor gave Hungary an early lead but a German fightback culminated in an 84th minute winner from Helmut Rahn. West Germany had won their first World Cup in the match dubbed the 'Miracle of Berne'.

West Germany also triumphed in the 1990 World Cup in Italy and on this day they met England in the semi-final that would produce one of the most iconic images of the tournament. With the scores level and the game into extra time, Paul Gascoigne was booked for a rash challenge, meaning he would miss the final if England got through. The image of his tear-stained eyes is one burned into the consciousness of every England fan.

JULY 5

When Enzo Bearzot included Paolo Rossi in his squad for the 1982 World Cup it was a massive gamble as he had not played competitive football for two years – the result of a ban after he got embroiled in a match fixing scandal at Perugia. He failed to score in the first three matches, but in the second round match on this day Rossi came alive and scored a hat-trick as Italy beat Brazil. He scored twice in the semi-final and bagged another in the 3-1 win over West Germany in the final. He had won the Golden Boot as top scorer, and Italy won the World Cup with Bearzot's decision vindicated in spectacular fashion.

Another Italian striker was having a less stellar time today in 1994. On this day, Gianfranco Zola started his only game of the 1994 World Cup and he marked his appearance on the biggest stage by getting sent off. Luckily for him Roberto Baggio scored twice as Italy went through to the final.

JULY 6

The 2006 World Cup was Sven-Göran Eriksson's last tournament as England boss and today in 2007 he began his post-England life when he was handed the managerial reins at Manchester City after Thaksin Shinawatra's takeover of the club. Despite doing better than anyone thought and finishing ninth in the Premiership, Sven was sacked after just one season in charge to the bafflement of City fans and the wider football world alike.

In 2009 Real Madrid smashed the world record transfer fee by splashing out £80m to lure Cristiano Ronaldo from Manchester United, and on this day, the latest *Galactico* signing was unveiled in front of 80,000 fans at the Bernabéu. 'I am just so happy to be here,' he said. 'For me, I have made my childhood dream a reality, which was nothing less than playing for Real Madrid.' He went on to spend nine years at the club, winning La Liga twice, and the Champions League four times.

JULY 7

Today in 1957 Edson Arantes do Nascimento announced his arrival as a top class footballer when he played his first match for his country, although no one would ever remember his name. Pelé was just 16 when he first played for Brazil in a match against Argentina. Although Brazil lost 2-1, Pelé scored on his debut for the senior side, three months before his 17th birthday.

While one great player began his international career today, another would end his on this day in 1990. Peter Shilton, one of England's best ever goalkeepers, played his final game for his country today in the third place play-off match against hosts Italy in the 1990 World Cup. Shilton captained the side that day but could not prevent the Italians winning 2-1.

JULY 8

Today in 1982 West Germany met France in the semi-finals of the World Cup – a match remembered for one of the worst fouls ever seen at the World Cup. West German goalkeeper Harald Schumacher flung himself into French defender Patrick Battiston, knocking him out cold and breaking two of his teeth. Referee Charles Corver didn't book Schumacher or even award the French a free kick.

Eight years later to the day, West Germany were in action in the 1990 World Cup final against Argentina. In the second half Argentine Pedro Monzón made history when he became the first player ever to be sent off in a World Cup final. Twenty minutes later Gustavo Dezotti was also given a red card. Andreas Brehme scored a late penalty to seal a 1-0 win for West Germany.

Germany were playing at the World Cup again on this day in 2014 – this time they humbled hosts Brazil 7-1 to silence the stunned crowd in Belo Horizonte, who couldn't believe what they were seeing. Unsurprisingly, Germany went on to lift the trophy, beating Argentina 1-0 in the final.

JULY 9

Today in 2001 Frenchman Zinedine Zidane became – at the time – the world's most expensive footballer ever when Spanish giants Real Madrid paid Juventus £45.8m to take him to the Bernabéu. The move reaped immediate rewards as Zidane helped the club win the European Cup in 2002 and La Liga the following season.

In April 2006 Zidane announced he would retire from football after the World Cup in Germany. Despite claims that he was well past his best, Zidane seemed revitalised at the tournament and dragged the France team to the final against Italy, which was played on this day. Zidane scored an early penalty and nearly won the match with a header that Buffon tipped over the crossbar. With penalties looming the world watched in astonishment as Zidane ran at Italian defender Marco Materazzi and headbutted him in the chest. It was his last act as a professional footballer as he was sent off and could only watch as France lost on penalties.

JULY 10

Henri Delaunay is not as well remembered as his contemporary Jules Rimet but Delaunay was also a strong proponent of the World Cup – and was the driving force behind the European Championship. The final of the first tournament took place today in 1960 in France with the USSR beating Yugoslavia 2-1 after extra time.

Exactly 56 years later to the day, the Euro 2016 final was held in Paris. Things looked bleak for Portugal when Cristiano Ronaldo was stretchered off midway through the first half, but try as they might, tournament hosts France couldn't find a goal. With penalties looming, Eder snuck a low shot past Hugo Lloris in the French goal to seal a 1-0 win for Portugal – and their first ever major trophy.

JULY 11

Today in the 1982 World Cup final Italian defender Marco Tardelli produced one of the most emotional goal celebrations ever seen after he scored from the edge of the area to give the Italians a 2-0 lead over West Germany. After the strike went in he sprinted towards the bench pumping his fists and shaking his head as he screamed 'Goal!' It became the enduring image of the tournament as Italy won their third World Cup.

England were knocked out of the 2018 World Cup semi-finals by Croatia on this day thanks to an extra-time goal from Mario Mandžukić, but three years later to the day the Three Lions had another chance of glory in the Euro 2020 final at Wembley. Things started brilliantly for Gareth Southgate's side who took the lead through Luke Shaw with just two minutes played, but Leonardo Bonucci equalised to set up another dreaded penalty shoot-out. Naturally, Italy won, and England's quest for a first trophy since 1966 continued.

JULY 12

On this day in 1974 the man revered as the greatest manager in Liverpool's history sent shockwaves across Merseyside when he unexpectedly resigned. In 15 years at Anfield, Bill Shankly transformed the club from a struggling Second Division side with a crumbling stadium and training ground to the greatest club side in England.

When Sir Alex Ferguson became manager at Manchester United he later stated his aim was to 'knock Liverpool right off their f***ing perch', and by the early 90s he had succeeded and achieved domestic dominance with his team. His attentions turned to Europe and today in 2001 he smashed the British transfer fee record when he spent £28m on Argentine Juan Sebastián Verón. He was supposed to be the player to cement United's position at the top of the European football tree, but he wasn't, and was sold to Chelsea at a £13m loss in 2003.

JULY 13

The first ever World Cup was held in Uruguay with the first two matches of the tournament held on this day in 1930 with France beating Mexico 4-1, and the USA defeating Belgium 3-0. Frenchman Lucien Laurent scored the first World Cup goal in history, 20 minutes into the game at the Estadio Gran Parque Central. Laurent later said: 'Everyone was pleased but we didn't all roll around on the ground – nobody realised that history was being made. A quick handshake and we got on with the game.'

Exactly 84 years later to the day and two of the giants of world football met in the World Cup final at the Maracanã Stadium in Rio de Janeiro. Mario Götze scored the only goal of the game as Germany beat Lionel Messi's Argentina to win the trophy for the fourth time.

JULY 14

It was called The Football War but the five-day conflict between El Salvador and Honduras that began on this day in 1969 had much deeper roots than football. Land reform and immigration issues were the real causes of the war but the rise in tensions coincided with the qualifying campaign for the 1970 World Cup. In the end a play-off match between the two nations would decide who would get to the finals. El Salvador won but the rioting between the two sets of fans was intense and within weeks El Salvador attacked Honduras until a ceasefire was struck after five days of violence.

On this day in 2005 Patrick Vieira left Arsenal to sign for Juventus for £13m. Most observers thought Arsene Wenger was mad to let his influential captain leave but the Arsenal boss saw that Vieira was past his peak and had Cesc Fàbregas waiting in the wings to slot into his midfield.

JULY 15

Today in 1989 a pioneering black player who racked up more firsts than Michael Schumacher had his life tragically cut short. Laurie Cunningham, nicknamed 'The Black Flash', was one of the first top black footballers in England and he achieved prominence playing for Ron Atkinson's West Bromwich Albion team in the 1970s. He went on to become not only Real Madrid's first Englishman, but also their first black player. He was also the first black player to represent England at any level, scoring on his debut for the under-21 team in 1977. He was killed in a car accident in Madrid aged just 33.

France claimed their second World Cup today in 2018 after beating Croatia 4-2 in the final at the Luzhniki Stadium in Moscow. A Mario Mandžukić own goal gave Les Bleus the lead after just 18 minutes with Antoine Griezmann, Paul Pogba and Kylian Mbappé adding to the scoreline.

JULY 16

'Everywhere has its irremediable national catastrophe, something like a Hiroshima. Our catastrophe, our Hiroshima was the defeat by Uruguay in 1950.' Nélson Rodrigues, Brazilian journalist. Today in 1950 saw possibly the biggest upset in international football history, a match that still scars the Brazilian consciousness to this day. Despite Uruguayan player Julio Pérez wetting himself during the national anthem, his team pulled off a stunning 2-1 victory on Brazilian soil. Goalkeeper Moacyr Barbosa in particular was blamed for the defeat. Before he died, penniless, in 2000, he remarked: 'Under Brazilian law the maximum sentence is thirty years. But my imprisonment has been fifty.'

The two South American rivals met again on this day in 1989 in the final of the Copa América. Brazil were going through a 19-year trophy dry spell but Romario scored the winner in this grudge match to end Brazil's barren run and exact a slice of revenge over Uruguay in the process.

July 17

Sky high players' wages, sky high ticket prices, and Sky Sports' incessant advertising of ever more climactic clashes between the top clubs – modern-day football in England and it all started today in 1991 with the signing of the Founder Members' Agreement. It was the blueprint for the Premier League, which enabled the top flight to negotiate its own TV and sponsorship deals independently from the rest of the Football League.

Despite all this new-found success for English clubs in the early 1990s, the national side was not doing so well. Under Graham Taylor England failed to qualify for the 1994 World Cup in the USA. Because of England's absence not everyone remembers much of the tournament but on this day Brazil won their fourth title, on penalties, at the expense of Italy, who had been dragged through to the final by Roberto Baggio, only for the Italian captain to miss the crucial penalty to hand the cup to Brazil.

July 18

International defenders across the globe were able to sleep a little better after today in 1971 after Pelé played his last game for Brazil, a 2-2 draw with Yugoslavia in Rio de Janeiro. In winning his 92 caps he scored 77 goals and picked up three World Cup winners' medals in the process.

Paul Ince was also causing a stir on this day back in 1997 when he left Internazionale for Liverpool in a £4m move. Having played with some distinction for Manchester United in the early 1990s he is one of the few players to cross the divide between the two clubs. Just to ram home the message that he was happy with his new team, after scoring an equaliser for Liverpool against United Ince celebrated wildly in front of the Kop, even kissing the Liverpool badge.

JOY AND DESPAIR. GOALKEEPER CLAUDIO TAFFAREL CELEBRATES BRAZIL'S WORLD CUP 1994 WIN AFTER ROBERTO BAGGIO MISSES HIS CRUCIAL PENALTY.

JULY 19

Sir Alf's boys and the Russian linesman were not the only heroes of 1966 as the plucky underdogs from North Korea managed to upset the form book with an amazing 1-0 victory over pre-tournament favourites Italy at Middlesbrough's Ayresome Park. The 1,000-1 rank outsiders' World Cup anthem included the unlikely boast, 'We can beat everyone, even the strongest team.' A Pak Doo-Ik goal and heroics from goalkeeper Ri Chan Myong meant they became the first ever Asian side to progress from the group stage at a World Cup.

Sixteen years after dropping out of the Premier League, Leeds United were finally promoted back to the big time. After financial ruin, a succession of controversial owners and countless doomed managers, it took the maverick genius of Marcelo Bielsa to drag the sleeping giant from its slumber in the pandemic-interrupted 2019/20 season. Today in 2020 saw a very hungover Leeds team pause what had been 48 hours of celebration since promotion had been confirmed to dispatch Derby County 3-1 at Pride Park.

JULY 20

On this day in 1871, in the offices of the *Sportsman* newspaper, the Football Association secretary, Charles Alcock said: 'It is desirable that a Challenge Cup should be established in connection with the Association, for which all clubs belonging to the Association should be invited to compete.' The FA Cup, the world's first national knockout tournament, was born. Alcock went on to captain the Wanderers team to victory in the first FA Cup final in 1872, and also captained England in a 2-2 draw with Scotland in 1875 – his only international appearance.

Another key event in the development of football as we know it also occurred on this day in 1885 when the FA, under pressure from leading clubs, legalised professional football. Some club chairmen had been breaking the rules for some time by offering wages to attract the best players so rather than fight against a growing trend the authorities decided to embrace change.

July 21

Today in 1964 a freak accident robbed football of one of its great players. Scotsman John White, a Tottenham Hotspur player under Bill Nicholson, was just 27 when he was struck by lightning while sheltering under a tree from a storm at Crews Hill golf course in Enfield. The man dubbed 'The Ghost' by the White Hart Lane faithful for his ability to appear unexpectedly in the opposition penalty area won the double in 1961 and was in the side when Spurs won the Cup Winners' Cup in 1963.

Nicholson paid £22,000 to bring White to Spurs – a lot of money in those days but dwarfed by the fees paid for players now. On this day in 1991 Italian club Bari paid £5.5m to Aston Villa for David Platt. One of only a handful of Englishmen to play at the top level abroad, Platt also notched up big money moves to Juventus, Sampdoria and Arsenal, taking his combined transfer fees to more than £22m – a record at the time.

July 22

On this day in 2002, Peter Ridsdale was forced to wake up from his dream and start facing reality at Leeds United. After missing out on the millions that Champions League qualification would have brought, Ridsdale had to balance the books somehow and sold club captain and record signing Rio Ferdinand to arch rivals Manchester United for £29.1m. Ferdinand's decision to cross the Pennines worked out well for him when he helped the club win the Premiership in his first season.

Arsenal got their first look at their new Emirates Stadium today in 2006 when the first match was held at the new ground. The first game was the last for Dennis Bergkamp in an Arsenal shirt as the Gunners took on Ajax in the Dutchman's testimonial. In 11 years at the club the BA Baracus of football (I ain't gettin' on no plane fool!) won the Premiership three times and the FA Cup four times.

JULY 23

The animosity between England and Argentina started on this day at the 1966 World Cup when the two nations met in the quarter-final at Wembley. It was a bad-tempered affair with Argentine captain Antonio Rattín eventually sent off. Incensed, he refused to leave the pitch for ten minutes before the match could restart. England won 1-0 and Alf Ramsey said: 'Our best football will come against the team which comes out to play football, and not to act as animals.'

Kevin Keegan played under Sir Alf for England towards the end of the manager's tenure. In February 1980 Keegan, who was European Footballer of the Year at the time, shocked the world by signing for Southampton. Today in that year KK made his debut for the Saints in a friendly against Shamrock Rovers at Lansdowne Road.

JULY 24

Today in 2000 Luís Figo was unveiled as the world's most expensive signing, as he put pen to paper for Real Madrid in a £38m transfer from bitter rivals Barcelona. His first visit back to Camp Nou was a fiery encounter with the home fans chanting 'Judas' throughout and pelting the pitch with missiles. In 2002 there was a repeat performance with even a severed pig's head thrown from the stands.

In 1998 Newcastle chairman Freddie Shepherd and director Douglas Hall were alienating their own fans when they were caught by the *News of the World*'s 'fake sheikh' Mazher Mahmood. They mocked their own club's supporters for spending vast amounts of money on merchandising, called female fans 'dogs' and described Alan Shearer as the 'Mary Poppins of football'. The pair were forced to stand down from the board but on this day in 1998 they voted themselves back on to it less than six months after their disgraceful exit.

JULY 25

When Walter Smith left Rangers in 1998 he did so with one of the best reputations in football management, having masterminded an incredible period of success for the club which saw them win nine consecutive league titles to equal Celtic's record. Today in 1998 he made his managerial debut south of the border when he took charge of Everton for the first time in a pre-season friendly. The result was a 1-1 draw with lowly Chester City.

Didier Drogba signed off his first stint with Chelsea by winning the Champions League for them with his last kick of the ball in Chelsea blue. Today in 2014, after spells in China and Turkey, Drogba re-signed for the club on a one-year deal.

JULY 26

When Bill Shankly shocked Liverpool by resigning in 1974 the fans went into mourning and few would have believed that the club was on the cusp of the greatest period in their history. Shanks' assistant Bob Paisley was announced as the new boss today in 1974 and the quiet coach who never really wanted the top job carried on where Shankly left off. In nine years as the gaffer he won an amazing 19 trophies including six league titles and three European Cups – he said once, 'Mind you, I've been here during the bad times too – one year we came second.'

It was today in 2006 that the Italian Football Federation (FIGC) announced its final rulings on the Calciopoli affair that rocked Italian football to the core. Juve were stripped of the two back-to-back titles they had just won, with the FIGC awarding the 2005/06 Scudetto to Internazionale and relegating Juve to Serie B in the process. Also indicted in the scandal were AC Milan, Fiorentina, Lazio and Reggina. Despite all this the national team still managed to win the 2006 World Cup.

JULY 27

When Jack Walker hired Kenny Dalglish as manager of Blackburn Rovers he told his new employee to go out and buy the best young talent in the country. The flagship signing of Uncle Jack's new Blackburn was the young Alan Shearer, who signed for the Lancashire club from Southampton today in 1992 for a then British record £3.6m. Dalglish later splashed the cash on Norwich City forward Chris Sutton and together the 'SAS' partnership of Shearer and Sutton would provide the goals to win the Premiership in 1995.

When Roman Abramovich bought Chelsea in 2003 he was labelled 'the new Jack Walker' because of his willingness to spend whatever it took to bring trophies to the club. Today in 2004 Roman sanctioned the signing of Portugal defender Ricardo Carvalho for just under £20m. The centre-back had been outstanding at Euro 2004 as Portugal reached the final and would help Chelsea win their first league title for 50 years in his first season at Stamford Bridge.

JULY 28

Today in 2006, striker Ruud van Nistelrooy was on the receiving end of a trademark ruthless move from the Manchester United boss Alex Ferguson when he sold the Dutchman to Real Madrid. Despite being incredibly prolific during his five year stint in Manchester, Ferguson was allegedly unhappy at his player's reaction to not starting the League Cup final against Wigan.

A less heralded transfer move occurred on the same day when Benni McCarthy swapped FC Porto for Blackburn Rovers. The striker who helped Porto win the European Cup under José Mourinho had been linked with a move to the Premiership with Everton, West Ham and Middlesbrough before Blackburn finally landed him for a fee thought to be around £2.5m.

JULY 29

As Europe lay in ruins after the Second World War, the powers that be decided to re-start the modern Olympic Games to give the world a much needed lift. Today in 1948 the Empire Stadium, better known as Wembley, was the venue for the opening ceremony of the games.

By the end of the century Wembley was ageing badly and a replacement was needed. Today in 1998 plans for a new national stadium on the Wembley site were unveiled. The new design, with its giant steel arch, was largely overshadowed by the revelation that the famous twin towers were not included in the design. A campaign to save them was unsuccessful and they were demolished in 2003.

JULY 30

It was a match that had everything: two fierce rival teams, plenty of goals, controversy, extra time and a pitch invasion. Oh, and it was the World Cup final at Wembley. It was on this day that the Three Lions roared their loudest and England reached the pinnacle of their footballing achievement by winning the World Cup in 1966. With a late equaliser from West Germany forcing extra time, England boss Sir Alf Ramsey told his troops: 'You've won it once. Now you'll have to go out there and win it again.' Geoff Hurst's controversial goal was given by the so-called Russian linesman Tofik Bakhramov (although he was actually from Azerbaijan), before Hurst made sure with a last-minute effort prompting commentator Kenneth Wolstenholme's famous words, 'There's some people on the pitch, they think it's all over.' Hurst then smacked the ball into the top corner to take the score to 4-2 and England to victory. 'It is now!' Wolstenholme added with brilliant timing.

Coincidentally it was also on this day that Uruguay defeated Argentina 4-2 to win the first ever World Cup in 1930.

JULY 31

Home to Sunderland and the famous 'Roker Roar' of the fans cheering on their team for 99 years, by the 1990s Roker Park's days were numbered. Following the Taylor Report and the need for all-seater stadia, the ageing ground was too small and the site too confined for expansion. The club built the Stadium of Light to replace it and today in 1997 Ajax were the opponents in the very first game at the gleaming new ground.

Newcastle United are of course Sunderland's bitter local rivals, and everyone on Tyneside and beyond was in mourning today in 2009 when former Toon boss Sir Bobby Robson passed away aged 76 after a long battle with cancer. Robson had a glittering managerial career at clubs including Ipswich, Porto and Barcelona – as well as an eight-year spell as England boss, when he took the Three Lions to the semi-finals at Italia 90.

FOOTBALL
On This Day

AUGUST

AUGUST 1

The regime of arguably England's worst ever manager kicked off today in 2006, when Steve McClaren turned up for his first day at Soho Square. In what was the shortest tenure of an England boss to date, McClaren would only last 16 months and 18 games before he was sent packing following the Three Lions' failure to qualify for Euro 2008.

Another manager was digging his heels in today in 1998 as Aston Villa boss John Gregory refused to sell Dwight Yorke to Manchester United. Gregory wanted Andy Cole in a swap deal, but Fergie had plans for the pair of them so wouldn't budge. Yorke took it upon himself to kick up a fuss, leading Gregory to say that 'If I'd had a gun I could have shot him.' Fergie easily won the brewing mind game as Yorke soon moved for a fee of £12.6m.

AUGUST 2

Sir Alex Ferguson once said that Dennis Wise could 'start a fight in an empty house', and today in 2002 Leicester City were agreeing with him, as they sacked the midfielder following his fracas with teammate Callum Davidson on the Foxes' pre-season tour of Finland. Davidson was acting as a peacemaker in a dispute between Wise and another unnamed player, receiving a broken nose and jaw for his troubles.

Arsene Wenger was eying reinforcements today in 1999 when he snapped up Croatian striker Davor Šuker from Real Madrid. The 31-year-old Šuker was a break from the norm for Wenger who was looking for experience to replace Nicolas Anelka, who had gone the other way to Real Madrid. Šuker never really hit off at Highbury, scoring 8 goals in 22 starts in his sole season at the club.

TOTTENHAM SPLASHED OUT £2M ON JÜRGEN KLINSMANN IN AUGUST 1994 (SEE OVER).

AUGUST 3

Despite being flummoxed by a nation that 'didn't put milk and sugar in their tea', John Charles today in 1957 became the first British professional to sign for an overseas club when he joined Juventus from Leeds United for a world record fee of £65,000. Charles was an instant hit: he was named Italian Player of the Year in his first season and in 1997 he was voted Serie A's greatest ever foreign player, ahead of Maradona, Platini, Van Basten and Zidane.

Jürgen Klinsmann was also dusting down his passport, as he joined Tottenham in 1994 following a £2m move from Monaco. The German was deeply unpopular in England following the 1990 World Cup and his reputation for play-acting, but soon won over the fans by poking fun at himself when he asked, 'Which way is it to the diving school? Ha!' in his first press conference. His trademark diving celebration was seen 21 times that season as he went on to win the Football Writers' Association Footballer of the Year award.

AUGUST 4

In a rare act of restraint Leeds United chairman Peter Ridsdale refused to succumb to Jimmy Floyd Hasselbaink's wage demands today in 1999 and sold him to Atlético Madrid for £12m. After being Leeds' top scorer for the last two years Jimmy was demanding that the club splashed out £60,000 a week for his services, which would have made him the highest paid player in the league. Jimmy's Mr 15 per cent got his way in the end though, as Atlético threw money at the striker but were promptly relegated that season.

The other half of Madrid was smarting today in 2000 when Ole Gunnar Solskjaer did what he used to do best and scored a last minute goal to give Manchester United a 1-0 victory over Real in the Centenary Tournament at the Olympic Stadium in Munich.

AUGUST 5

Not many English fans will be celebrating the first appearance of the penalty shoot-out on these shores that came about in 1970 when Manchester United and Hull couldn't be separated in the long-forgotten Watney Mann Invitational Cup. George Best was the first to step up as he dispatched his spot kick at Boothferry Park and although Denis Law became the first British player to miss, United still went on to win 4-3.

Roman Abramovich proved that he was pretty serious about this football lark today in 2003 when he got out his chequebook and signed up the midfield pairing of Joe Cole and Juan Sebastián Verón for £6.6m and £15m respectively. Cole had just been relegated with West Ham and proved to be a shrewd signing, but the Argentine Verón flopped, making only 14 appearances for Chelsea. Manchester United would've laughed all the way to the bank if they hadn't paid £28.1m for him two years earlier.

AUGUST 6

Sheffield Wednesday moved quickly today in 1999 to denounce claims by their cross-town rivals United that the two clubs should merge following heavy financial losses. Blades chairman John Thurman seemed to leave common sense at the door as he talked up the benefits of the two rivals teaming up, much to the chagrin of pretty much everyone else in the city.

Fergie revealed that he liked an impulse buy on holiday as much as the rest of us in 2003 after Manchester United's 3-1 friendly defeat to Sporting Lisbon. Cristiano Ronaldo had impressed the United players so much that they badgered their boss to sign the 18-year-old on the flight back after he had created two goals and run riot. A week later United agreed a £12m deal for the winking Portuguese.

AUGUST 7

A section of Millwall fans proved that the club's reputation for trouble was well founded when they used the new-fangled internet to organise a mass brawl with Cardiff fans following the two sides' meeting in 1999. This was the first time that football hooliganism had gone online, with one site even posting a running commentary of events in Cardiff's café quarter that caused the district to virtually close down for two hours.

There must have been something in the air that day, as 300 miles up north at St James' Park Alan Shearer was getting sent off for the first time in his career. Uriah Rennie dismissed the England captain following a second-half foul on Aston Villa's Ian Taylor.

AUGUST 8

On the eve of the Premiership's first season Leeds and Liverpool played out the 1992 Charity Shield at Wembley, with an Eric Cantona hat-trick inspiring Leeds to a 4-3 win. This was to be one of the mercurial Frenchman's last contributions for the Yorkshire side as he would up and leave for Manchester United two months later, with Leeds' hopes of defending their title going with him as they finished the season in 17th place.

There was another major footballing split in 1999 as it was announced that Gary Lineker was taking over as the host of *Match of the Day* from Des Lynam. Dishy Des had ruled the roost on the programme for 11 years but jumped ship to join ITV, leaving crisp-enthusiast Lineker to take up the mantle of the housewives' favourite.

AUGUST 9

Bradford City laid down a statement of intent today in 2000 when they snapped up striker Benito Carbone. Although the livewire Italian was a free transfer, the Bantams were reportedly paying him £40,000 a week as they began to live beyond their means in an effort to maintain their place in the Premier League. Two years later the club found themselves in administration as they began to drop down the leagues as players such as Carbone were still picking up their Premier League-sized pay packets.

In 1998 Dion Dublin got Coventry City off to the best possible start when he bagged a hat-trick in their opening game against Chelsea. The Sky Blues were following up an 11th place finish from the season before and Dublin bounced back from the disappointment of missing out on England's World Cup squad in style.

AUGUST 10

Sir Alex Ferguson eventually lost patience with party animal Lee Sharpe today in 1996, selling him to Leeds United for £4.5m. The 'Sharpey shuffle' goal celebration was in short supply at Elland Road though, as injuries and loss of form saw him only turn out 30 times in two years for Leeds. After that, he slipped down the divisions and ended up as a reality television star on *Celebrity Love Island*, a show that comedian Steve Merchant watched whilst 'praying for a tsunami'.

Another high-profile career was hitting the rocks today in 2003 when Arsenal's Francis Jeffers was sent off in the Community Shield only 15 minutes after coming on as a sub. One of Wenger's rare misses in the transfer market, he was signed in 2001 as a 'fox in the box' for £9m, but struggled to live up to the hype and was shipped off back to Everton on loan by the end of the month.

AUGUST 11

In 2006 Steve McClaren was ten days into his England regime, so decided it was time to distance himself from his predecessor and drop Sven's favourite, David Beckham, for his first game against Greece. Reaction to the move was mixed, although many thought that Beckham was still a useful enough player to keep in the squad, but McClaren stood firm... for a while. Following some indifferent performances from the England team, 'Golden Balls' was back by the end of the season as McClaren began to look like he was out of his depth.

Ten years earlier Alan Shearer was making his debut for Newcastle United in the Charity Shield, where the Toon were on the wrong side of a 4-0 drubbing at the hands of Manchester United. Shearer had recently turned down Fergie's advances to join his hometown club in a record £15m move from Blackburn.

AUGUST 12

Sandwiched in between the title-winning reigns of George Graham and Arsène Wenger was Bruce Rioch, who was sacked by Arsenal today in 1996 after a dispute over transfer funds. He may not have picked up any silverware during his time at Highbury, but his Bergkamp-shaped legacy put his successor in good stead.

Former Arsenal legend David O'Leary showed he wasn't afraid to splash the big bucks today in 1999 when the Leeds manager snapped up Coventry striker Darren Huckerby for £5.5m. O'Leary seemed to have something of a striker fetish though and also signed Robbie Keane, Robbie Fowler, Michael Bridges and Mark Viduka over the next couple of seasons to add to home-grown frontman Alan Smith and Australian Harry Kewell.

AUGUST 13

After the Berlin Olympics had put Nazi Germany in the international spotlight, Adolf Hitler decided that the only way to surpass the success of this event was to bid for the World Cup, so today in 1936 Germany applied to host the 1942 edition. Keen to seize upon football's mass popular appeal and exploit it as a vehicle for Nazi propaganda, Hitler ignored the fact that the finals had already been promised to Brazil. In the end it proved academic as he saw invading Europe and starting the Second World War as a better way to assert his power.

Andriy Shevchenko made his Chelsea debut in the Community Shield today in 2006 following his £30m move from AC Milan. Although he managed to score in their 2-1 loss to Liverpool he soon found the going tough in England, prompting journalist James Richardson to quip that: 'Chelsea paid a levy for the Shevy but the Shevy went dry.'

AUGUST 14

Kevin Keegan got his Liverpool career off to a winning start today in 1971 when he scored 12 minutes into his debut against Nottingham Forest. Six trophy-packed and often controversial years at Anfield followed where Kopites were treated to 100 goals in 323 appearances and some of the best hair-dos the 70s had to offer.

Coming in at the other end of the hair spectrum is follically-challenged Tommy Mooney, who silenced the Kop in 1999 as newly-promoted Watford pulled off a shock 1-0 win against Liverpool. The good times didn't last long for the Hornets though, as they would end the season bottom of the table. Mooney meanwhile got his journeyman on, roaming the lower leagues before fancying a spell in the sun, signing for UD Marbella in 2008.

AUGUST 15

A revolution in English football came roaring on to our screens today in 1992 as the newly re-branded Premiership kicked off. In theory, we had the same teams and the same players as we did in the plain ol' First Division, but Sky threw flashy new graphics, cheerleaders and ever increasing amounts of dosh at the game. Whereas the BBC and ITV showed highlights and the occasional live game, fans now had more live matches than they could shake a stick at.

Brian Deane was the first player to score in the Premiership, when he struck in the fifth minute of Sheffield United's 2-1 win over Manchester United to secure his place in the history books forevermore. Despite this early loss, the Red Devils managed to pick themselves up and win the first Premiership title nine months later.

AUGUST 16

For all the big names and egos in the all-conquering Manchester United team of the 1990s, quiet man Denis Irwin was just as important to the club's success. The Irish full-back was granted a testimonial today in 2000 against local rivals Manchester City, but it seems that City boss Joe Royle forgot to tell his charges that it was only a friendly. City new-boy George Weah made a clumsy challenge on Irwin early in the game, causing him to be stretchered off.

Glenn Hoddle's mouth was getting him in more trouble today in 2003 when he claimed that he knew 'from the first minute' that decisions would go against his team in Tottenham's clash with Birmingham City. Hoddle objected to the appointment of Rob Styles for the opening day Premier League match, as he believed that Styles was trying to 'balance things up' after he sent off a Birmingham player during a pre-season game.

AUGUST 17

After a year of establishing his place in the Manchester United team David Beckham became a household name today in 1996 when he scored a long-range effort against Wimbledon. After picking the ball up in his own half, Beckham looked up, saw Neil Sullivan off his line and lofted a right-foot shot over the furiously back-pedalling Scottish keeper. A few weeks later Beckham won his first England cap and he went on to win the PFA Young Player of the Year award that season.

Another England star was taking his first steps on the way to stardom today in 2002, as Wayne Rooney started his first Premier League game for Everton. The 17-year-old wasted no time in making his mark, setting up a goal in the Toffeemen's 2-2 opening day draw with Tottenham.

AUGUST 18

Blackburn Rovers fans were in mourning today in 2000 as chairman Jack Walker died, aged 71. After making his fortune in the steel industry Walker lived the dream of every football fan. He invested millions in his hometown club, bringing a new stadium, promotion and even the Premier League title to Ewood Park all within four years of buying the club in 1991.

Manchester United thought they had their own benefactor today in 1989 when it was announced that Michael Knighton had agreed to buy the club for £20m in what would have then been the biggest takeover deal in British football history. Knighton even went as far as appearing on the Old Trafford pitch before a game, dressed in full kit to show his keepy-uppy skills off to the crowd before his backers pulled out and he had to settle for taking over Carlisle United instead.

AUGUST 19

We all like to make brash predictions when we're talking footy, which normally leads to a ribbing and loss of a fiver amongst your mates. Imagine how embarrassing it would be if millions of people were watching though? Alan Hansen knows exactly how this feels, as he today in 1995 announced on *Match of the Day* that 'you'll never win anything with kids', after a young Manchester United side lost the season opener to Aston Villa 3-1. Needless to say United romped to the title that year and the Scot was left with egg on his face.

Another youngster making headlines today in 1999 was Robbie Keane who became the most expensive teenager in British football when he left Wolves to join Coventry for £6m. He trumped this move a year later when he joined Ronaldo and Christian Vieri up front for Internazionale for £13m, but would only turn out six times for the Nezazzurri.

AUGUST 20

It was a transfer that no one saw coming. What was the most glamorous club in the world doing buying an injury-prone convicted criminal for £13.4 million to marshal their defence? Yes, it was on this day in 2004 that Jonathan Woodgate completed his move from Newcastle to Real Madrid. Woodgate's first season at the Bernabeu was an injury-hit washout and the defender didn't make his debut until September 2005, when he scored an own goal and was sent off. 'It was not the best start in the world,' he would later deadpan.

Twelve months after being crowned European champions, Sarina Wiegman's England took on Spain in the World Cup final in Sydney today in 2023, looking to replicate the success of Sir Alf Ramsey's 1966 side. Alas, it would be one step too far for the Lionesses as Olga Carmona's first-half goal proved to be the difference. A brilliant penalty save from Mary Earps proved to be the English highlight of a final in which the Spaniards deservedly triumphed.

AUGUST 21

Classic pub quiz fodder today, as we let you know who the first player was to come on as a substitute in a league match. In 1965 Bolton were taking on Charlton at Burnden Park when Addicks keeper Mike Rose went down injured and was replaced by Keith Peacock, father of former QPR and Chelsea midfielder and purveyor of silly facial hair Gavin. After a re-shuffle John Hewie went in goal and was unable to prevent Bolton winning 4-2.

Football and politics collided in Northern Ireland today in 2002 as Neil Lennon withdrew from the national side's squad to play Cyprus. Lennon had received death threats following his alleged claim that he wanted to play in a united Ireland team. After 40 caps, the Northern Ireland captain announced his retirement from the team.

AUGUST 22

The grand old institution that is *Match of the Day* made its debut today in 1964. Kenneth Wolstenholme greeted the 20,000 viewers on BBC Two with highlights of Liverpool's 3-2 win over Arsenal. Within a couple of years over five million were tuning in to hear that iconic theme tune every week. The programme is still going strong today, although thanks to Mr Lineker and company there are far more dodgy puns than there were in the 60s.

Bradford City fans were no doubt crowding round their televisions for *MOTD* today in 2000 as they beat Chelsea 2-0 to raise hopes that their second season in the Premier League would be as memorable as their first. Chelsea boss Gianluca Vialli complained that his side couldn't cope with their opponents' 'unbearable tempo', but alas, it would not last and the Bantams were soon staring down the barrel of the relegation gun.

AUGUST 23

Man City's Ben Thatcher laid down his challenge to Maggie for the title of 'hardest Thatcher' today in 2006 when he threw his iron elbow at Portsmouth midfielder Pedro Mendes, leaving him out cold and in need of oxygen and hospital treatment. After the Welsh international was only given a yellow card for his blatant attack on Mendes, Pompey manager Harry Redknapp pondered: 'What do you have to do to get a red, kill someone?' The FA did see sense in the end, giving him an eight match ban.

Newcastle attempted to lay down a marker of their intent for the coming season and keep their oh-so demanding fans happy when they made a £20m bid for Everton's Wayne Rooney today in 2004. Whilst no one with an ounce of common sense believed the move would go ahead, it kept the Toon in the headlines and gave the rest of the football world a chance to have a laugh at them.

AUGUST 24

Ruud Gullit made one of the most foolish decisions he could have made as Newcastle United manager today in 1999 when he left Alan Shearer on the bench for their match at home to local rivals Sunderland. Newcastle were not enjoying a good start to the season and when they went down 2-1 to the Mackems he was bright enough to realise he wasn't wanted and quit three days later.

In 1957 another goal-getter was making the headlines as a 17-year-old Jimmy Greaves marked his Chelsea debut with a goal against Tottenham. Jimmy had a thing about debuts: he also struck on his first appearances for AC Milan, Spurs and West Ham as well as on his under-21 and full England debuts as he went on to notch an incredible 422 goals for club and country.

AUGUST 25

Middlesbrough was the unlikely location that pint-sized Brazilian midfielder Juninho landed at today in 1995. Boro had just achieved promotion into the Premier League and splashed out £4.75m on the 22-year-old. The 'Little Fella', as he was dubbed by fans, was an instant success on Teeside, but could not prevent his side from being relegated in 1997. Despite not fancying the First Division and leaving for Atlético Madrid, he had two further spells at the club, thereby cementing his place as one the city's favourite sons.

He may have been lacking in silky Brazilian skills, but Bobby Langton fired his way into the history books today in 1948 when he scored the quickest ever goal, striking after seven seconds for Preston against Manchester City. During his career Langton won seven England caps, but failed to reproduce his domestic form, only bagging one goal for his country.

AUGUST 26

As everyone's favourite dour scouser came home today in 1993 his wife no doubt broke into a chorus of 'Cheer Up Peter Reid'. Her man had just been sacked as Manchester City manager after three years in charge at Maine Road. Reidy had lost his first managerial job after his Man City side resorted to long-ball tactics and subsequently dropped down the table.

Meanwhile down in west London in 2003 Roman Abramovich continued his initial splurge on new recruits, bringing in Hernán Crespo from Internazionale for £16.8m. Formerly the world's most expensive player after his £35.5m move from Parma to Lazio, Crespo never really hit the heights at Stamford Bridge, scoring 20 goals in between loan spells at Inter and AC Milan.

AUGUST 27

Another day, another Newcastle managerial casualty. Kenny Dalglish won the 1998/99 sack race when he was dismissed only two games into the season. King Kenny had found the Newcastle job a tad harder than his last two posts, as he didn't inherit a star-studded squad as he did at Liverpool and didn't have Jack Walker's millions to spend. Newcastle had finished the previous season in 13th place, and a bad start to the new season was the final nail in his coffin.

A year earlier, Dennis Bergkamp scored one of the greatest hat-tricks ever seen, in Arsenal's 3-3 draw with Leicester at Filbert Street. His third was a sublime strike, as the Dutchman controlled a 40-yard pass with ease, juggled it past Spencer Prior then slotted it home, all in just four touches. Two of these strikes helped Bergkamp become the first player to bag the top three spots in *Match of the Day*'s Goal of the Month competition.

AUGUST 28

What did you achieve in the last 4 minutes and 33 seconds? We'd like to hedge a bet that it wasn't as productive as Robbie Fowler's antics today in 1994 when he scored – at the time – the fastest ever Premiership hat-trick against Arsenal. While Fowler's career somewhat stalled after his first spell at Liverpool, it's worth remembering that in his youth he was frequently hailed as the best finisher of his generation.

In 1989 Alex Ferguson decided that the key to ending United's title drought was throwing money at a top-class defender. It was on this day that he set his sights on Middlesbrough rock Gary Pallister, breaking the transfer record between two English clubs and paying £2.3m for the uncompromising centre-back as the foundations for the club's renaissance were being put into place.

AUGUST 29

If you ever need to be reminded what a fickle bunch most football fans are, then cast your mind back to today in 1998. David Beckham was playing his first away game for Manchester United following his red card against Argentina in the World Cup. Death threats, abuse from the terraces and even effigies were in abundance, as Becks got his head down and played his way back into the nation's favour.

A truly grim 10 days for football culminated in the death of Zambian international Chaswe Nsofwa today in 2007 whilst playing a training match. Nsofwa's death from a heart attack came in the immediate aftermath of Sevilla's Antonio Puerta and Walsall's 16-year-old Anton Reid dying on the pitch and QPR's 18-year-old striker Ray Jones' death in a car crash. Another player, Clive Clarke, on loan at Leicester, suffered two heart failures in the changing room the day before, but was stabilised before being taken to hospital.

AUGUST 30

Glenn Hoddle once said that Andy Cole needed five chances to score a goal. We can't even begin to fathom how many chances he had today in 1999 when the then Manchester United striker managed to put four past his old club Newcastle United in the Red Devils' 5-1 demolition job of their old rivals as they began their march on to yet another league title. Newcastle meanwhile, were struggling to make sense of it all following Ruud Gullit's recent departure.

Jetting into Manchester four years later was Steve McManaman, who ended his four-year stay at Real Madrid by joining up with his former England boss Kevin Keegan at Manchester City. His spell in Spain had seen him establish himself as one of the best English exports in recent years.

AUGUST 31

This day in 2004 saw Wayne Rooney make a mockery of the 'Once a Blue, Always a Blue' t-shirt he showed off to the world at Goodison Park as the Everton youngster became a red, signing for Manchester United for £27m. He went on to win every club trophy going in his 13-year spell at Old Trafford, before returning to Everton in 2017.

One of the most baffling transfer deadline day deals in the Premier League era was the arrival of Carlos Tévez and Javier Mascherano at West Ham in 2006. The two Argentine stars had been courted by some of Europe's biggest clubs, but left Corinthians for the Boleyn Ground in mysterious circumstances. This in turn led to one of football's most tiresome legal battles, as questions were raised over the third-party ownership of the pair and bored the pants off everyone.

FOOTBALL
On This Day

SEPTEMBER

SEPTEMBER 1

Brothers Paul and Oliver Collyer have got a lot to answer for. Exams have been failed, relationships have ended and social lives ruined thanks to them. On this day in 1992 they unleashed the first edition of *Championship Manager*, the annoyingly addictive football simulation computer game. You tell yourself you'll only play for half an hour but suddenly you notice you haven't left your desk for nine hours as you find yourself on the cusp of promotion to the Premiership, with that Norwegian left-back you been tracking about to sign and simply can't tear yourself away.

Today in 2001 England achieved a result that would have been more believable on a computer game when they thrashed Germany 5-1 in Munich in a World Cup qualifier. One of Sven-Göran Eriksson's early games in charge, he was hailed as a genius as even Emile Heskey managed to score in the rout, with a Michael Owen hat-trick and a Steven Gerrard strike completing the scoring.

SEPTEMBER 2

It was on this day in 1986 that Matt Le Tissier made his Southampton debut at the Dell against Tottenham. Saints won the match 2-0 and although Matt himself didn't score, it was not long before he was off the mark, scoring against Manchester United later in the year. Nicknamed Le God by Saints fans, Le Tissier was one of the most gifted players of his generation and made a habit of scoring spectacular goals. Despite the overtures of a host of Europe's top clubs including AC Milan, Chelsea, Liverpool and Tottenham, Le Tissier never left Southampton and in over 500 club appearances he scored 209 goals.

A notable date today in 2017 for Billericay Town, one of the more interesting non-league 'projects' in recent years. New owner Glenn Tamplin tooled up the Isthmian League side with the likes of Jamie O'Hara, Jermaine Pennant and Paul Konchesky and today in 2017 began an FA Cup campaign that would see them reach the first round proper with a 5-0 first qualifying round win over Didcot Town. During his ownership Tamplin would twice hire – and fire – himself as manager before stepping down as owner in 2019.

SEPTEMBER 3

Before the move to north London, Woolwich Arsenal was a bit of a yo-yo club, flitting between the top two divisions. On this day in 1904 they played their first ever top-flight match after winning promotion the previous season. Their first fixture was a long trek to Newcastle United where they lost 3-0.

Today in 1999 Bobby Robson realised a lifelong ambition when he was appointed Newcastle manager at the age of 66. Sir Bobby had already turned the job down once when he did not want to break his contract with Barcelona to replace Kevin Keegan. He was the oldest boss in the Premiership and sounded a lot like Clive Dunn from *Dad's Army* at his first press conference. 'I have got a massive job ahead of me. It's a great challenge and I am up for it. There is no need for panic here,' he said.

SEPTEMBER 4

Today in 1867 at a meeting at the Adelphi Hotel in Sheffield, one of England's biggest clubs was founded. Originally known as The Wednesday, Sheffield Wednesday was, like a lot of football clubs, born out of the need to keep the cricketers fit over the winter. The team originally played at Bramall Lane and the Olive Grove but in 1900 moved to their current home – Hillsborough – in the Owlerton area, which is how they got their nickname the Owls.

It was on this day in 1998 that fans everywhere were all grimacing together, regardless of club, when Liverpool defender Phil Babb clattered into the goal post with his legs either side of it. He was desperately trying to prevent Chelsea's Pierluigi Casiraghi from scoring after he had gone around Liverpool keeper David James. Sliding across the turf, Babb missed the ball, which rolled into the net for a goal, while Babb himself came to an abrupt stop when he 'tackled' the goal post.

SEPTEMBER 5

Paul Gascoigne could have joined either Manchester United or Tottenham Hotspur when he left Newcastle but he was lured to White Hart Lane by Terry Venables' promise that joining Spurs would get him in the England team. He was right and on this day in 1988 Bobby Robson gave Gazza his first call-up to the senior team. He made his debut at Wembley in the 1-0 win over Denmark a few days later.

Gazza and Venables had long since departed when Christian Gross became Spurs manager. He had arrived waving a London Underground ticket claiming it would be the ticket to his dreams, but flirtation with relegation meant he lasted little more than one season before on this day in 1998 Alan Sugar, no doubt flanked by his sidekicks Nick and Margaret, called Gross into his boardroom, wrinkled his brow, pointed at the unfortunate Swiss and growled: 'You're fired!'

SEPTEMBER 6

Today in 1989 England played Sweden away in a World Cup qualification game which was largely unremarkable except for the contribution of one man. Centre-half Terry Butcher took a head injury early on in the match but after some impromptu stitching up from the medical staff he carried on. By continuing to head the ball time and again he split open the wound which was bleeding throughout the game. By the end of the match his white England shirt was covered in blood – an iconic image of the spirit of the man.

On this day in 1995 Colombia were England's opponents at Wembley with the 0-0 friendly memorable for the antics of the Colombian goalkeeper René Higuita. Nicknamed 'El Loco' by his countrymen, Higuita pulled off his infamous scorpion kick save from a Jamie Redknapp long-range effort in this match.

COLOMBIAN GOALKEEPER RENE HIGUITA PULLED OFF HIS FAMOUS SCORPION SAVE IN SEPTEMBER 1995 AT WEMBLEY.

SEPTEMBER 7

England had a distinct look of red about them today in 1977 when they lined up at Wembley for a friendly against Switzerland with no fewer than six Liverpool players in the starting 11, plus Kevin Keegan who had only just left Anfield to try his luck on the continent. Terry McDermott made his debut alongside clubmates Ian Callaghan, Ray Clemence, Emlyn Hughes, Ray Kennedy and Phil Neal.

Four years later Clemence, Neal, Keegan and McDermott were all in the England team that lost 2-1 away to Norway. The defeat prompted one of the most famous pieces of commentary ever from Norwegian Bjorge Lillelien who went berserk screaming: 'Lord Nelson! Lord Beaverbrook! Sir Winston Churchill! Sir Anthony Eden! Clement Attlee! Henry Cooper! Lady Diana! Maggie Thatcher – can you hear me, Maggie Thatcher! Your boys took one hell of a beating! Your boys took one hell of a beating!'

SEPTEMBER 8

On this day in 1888 the first matches of the revolutionary new Football League were played. William McGregor, a Scot who was a director of Aston Villa, had come up with the idea of a league to introduce some order into what was then a chaotic world of cup and friendly fixtures. The first season saw 12 teams compete for the title: Preston North End, Bolton Wanderers, Everton, Burnley, Accrington, Blackburn Rovers, Aston Villa, West Bromwich Albion, Wolverhampton Wanderers, Notts County, Derby County and Stoke. Sadly, records are patchy on who was the first ever league goalscorer, with most people's best guess being Jack Gordon of Preston North End, who would go on to be champions.

The death of Queen Elizabeth II today in 2022 saw all football from the Premier League down to grassroots postponed in England, Wales, Scotland and Northern Ireland. The Queen had been a patron of the FA and during the early years of her reign would be a regular at Wembley finals, handing Bobby Moore the World Cup trophy in 1966 and presenting the FA Cup trophy to victorious captains 11 times.

SEPTEMBER 9

Yet another sign that football was increasingly becoming as much about business as it was pleasure was seen on this day in 1998 when Manchester United confirmed to the London Stock Exchange that it had accepted a bid of £623.4m from Rupert Murdoch's BSkyB television company. The fans were aghast and thought the club was selling its soul. They found an unlikely hero in the government's trade secretary Stephen Byers, who blocked the sale.

On the very same day the club took on Charlton in a Premiership match at Old Trafford. Expected demonstrations against Murdoch largely failed to materialise with only a handful of banners in protest at the proposed takeover. Any negative feelings were soon banished by a superb display by United who won 4-1, with new record signing Andy Cole bagging a brace on his debut to immediately start repaying his £7m fee.

SEPTEMBER 10

Today in 1898 Sunderland's Roker Park stadium was officially opened by the president of the club, Charles Stewart Vane-Tempest-Stewart, The Marquis of Londonderry, before an inaugural match against Liverpool which the home side won 1-0 thanks to a James Leslie goal six minutes from time. The ground would be the home of Sunderland for nearly 100 years, after which the club moved to the Stadium of Light in 1997.

Well-travelled goalkeeper Dave Beasant never played for Sunderland or Liverpool, but they were about the only clubs he didn't turn out for at some stage in his hobo-like career. Today in 2002, the player most famous for injuring himself by dropping a jar of salad cream on his foot signed for Bradford City. At the time it was his 11th club but he would rack up another three before he retired.

SEPTEMBER 11

Everyone knows the World Cup was stolen in 1966 and eventually found by a dog named Pickles, but it is not the only football trophy to be pinched in England. Today in 1895 the first FA Cup trophy, known as the 'little tin idol' was stolen from a shop in Birmingham where it was on display after Aston Villa had won the competition. Despite the offer of a £10 reward the cup was never recovered, so Villa had to pay £25 for a replacement. Some 63 years later a petty criminal named Harry Burge claimed he had stolen it and melted it down to make counterfeit half-crown coins.

On this day in 2000 Australian firm Multiplex signed a contract to build the new Wembley Stadium for a maximum price of £326.5m. The project was dogged with problems and delays and was eventually finished four years late at a cost of £798m.

SEPTEMBER 12

By the summer of Euro 92 and England's last game of the tournament, Gary Lineker could not even bring himself to look at Graham Taylor when the England boss substituted the striker, thereby denying him the chance to equal Bobby Charlton's record of 49 goals for England. The two were altogether happier today in 1990 when Taylor named Lineker as his captain for his first game as England boss – a 1-0 win over Hungary at Wembley, with Lineker scoring.

'I fell in love with football as I was later to fall in love with women: suddenly, inexplicably, uncritically, giving no thought to the pain or disruption it would bring with it.' So is the opening line of Nick Hornby's excellent book, *Fever Pitch*, which was first published today in 1992. It was the football book everyone thought they could have written about themselves, which was just an indication of how well it encapsulated the realities of being a football fan.

SEPTEMBER 13

Today in 1997, Arsenal striker Ian Wright scored a hat-trick against Bolton at Highbury to break Cliff Bastin's record as the club's record goalscorer. Bastin's record of 178 goals had stood for fifty years but Wright's record would only stand for eight when Thierry Henry overtook him in October 2005. The Frenchman eventually scored 226 goals for the club before va va vooming to Barcelona.

On this day in 2004 Newcastle United continued their increasingly desperate search for a manager to bring them some success when they appointed Graeme Souness to replace the sacked Sir Bobby Robson. Robson had lifted the club after the ill-fated Ruud Gullit reign but a series of discipline problems and wavering form were enough for chairman Freddy Shepherd to fire him. Souness came in with a reputation as a disciplinarian but did little to take the club forward despite spending £50m. He was sacked in February 2006.

SEPTEMBER 14

The humble penalty kick: scourge of England, mastered by Germany, and invented by an Irishman named William McCrum. A Victorian mill owner and goalkeeper from Milford in Co Armagh, McCrum came up with the idea to stop cheating and eventually the Football League in England introduced it to the game. Today in 1891 John Heath of Wolverhampton Wanderers scored the first ever Football League penalty in a 5-0 thrashing of Accrington Stanley at Molineux.

On this day in 1963 Northern Irishman George Best made his debut for Manchester United in a 1-0 win over West Bromwich Albion. Two years earlier Sir Matt Busby had received a telegram from Bob Bishop, one of his scouts. It read: 'I think I've found you a genius.' The performer had found his stage and Bestie would grace Old Trafford for the next ten spellbinding years which would see him, and United, at their peak.

SEPTEMBER 15

Derby County was one of England's top clubs in the 1970s. Brian Clough had dragged them out of the Second Division in 1969 and had won them the title by 1972. Their first season in Europe the following year saw an exhilarating run to the semi-finals only to be denied by Juventus or 'the cheating bastards' as Cloughie termed them after the match. Ol' Big 'Ead left in 1973 but on this day in 1976 the club were still flying high and put 12 goals past the Irish team Finn Harps in a 16-1 aggregate victory. Not that it did them much good as AEK Athens knocked them out in the next round.

He was dispensed with just one season after Roman Abramovich's arrival at Chelsea but it was on this day in 2000 that former owner Ken Bates installed Claudio Ranieri as manager at Stamford Bridge. Cantona-like, Ranieri said: 'I was flattered by the call. If there are roses they will bloom.'

SEPTEMBER 16

Today in 1937, football first flirted with television – the start of a blossoming marriage that means now, thanks to Sky, you can barely go a single day without a match being screened. The BBC had started their new-fangled television service in 1936 and decided it might lend itself quite well to the beautiful game, so a specially organised match between Arsenal and Arsenal reserves was held to test out the new technology.

More than sixty years later and millions watched Manchester United take on Barcelona at Old Trafford in the Champions League. Despite being 2-0 up United fell apart in the second half, having Nicky Butt sent off and eventually settling for a 3-3 draw. United would of course have the last laugh that season though when they lifted the trophy at Barcelona's home ground the following May in their remarkable treble season.

SEPTEMBER 17

The only club ever to sack Sir Alex Ferguson is St Mirren; the Scottish minnows gave him the boot in 1978 but the nucleus of the squad he built continued to flourish after he had left for Aberdeen. They finished third in the Scottish First Division in the 1979/80 season, earning them a first ever foray into Europe. Their first tie was on this day in 1980 against Sweden's IF Elfsborg, which they won 2-1. They were put out in the following round and have not qualified for Europe since.

Chelsea have long been a club with a European flavour about them but on this day in 2000 their foreign legion team, containing just three Englishman, lost 2-0 at Stamford Bridge to a Leicester team made up entirely of British-born players. It was Claudio Ranieri's first match in charge and his new team were undone by goals from Muzzy Izzet and Stan Collymore.

SEPTEMBER 18

Before all-seater stadia, thousands more fans could squeeze into the grounds and today in 1948 the record attendance at a Merseyside derby was set when 78,299 scousers packed into Goodison Park to watch Everton take on Liverpool. It is also the record attendance for any league match at Everton's home ground.

They say you have to be mad to be a goalkeeper and Bruce Grobbelaar was madder than most. Today in 1998 the wobbly-legged Liverpool keeper was charged with betting irregularities by the FA. The *Sun* had broken the story and had a video of Grobbelaar accepting a £2,000 down payment, discussing future games that he was going to throw and lamenting other matches where he had accidentally made saves that had cost him thousands of pounds from his Far East betting syndicate. Relying on evidence from former Arsenal keeper Bob Wilson, Grobbelaar just managed to avoid prosecution.

SEPTEMBER 19

Newcastle United fans really were walking in a Robson wonderland today in 1999 when, in his first game in charge of the club, Bobby Robson's new team ran out 8-0 winners over Sheffield Wednesday with Toon hero Alan Shearer bagging five goals himself. Aaron Hughes, Kieron Dyer and Gary Speed got the other goals in the rout. After the match Shearer showed the sort of enthusiasm that makes his punditry less than exciting, saying: 'We must not get carried away. I'm sorry to bring everybody down to earth.'

Former Tottenham and England great Jimmy Greaves passed away today in 2021 at the age of 81. His Three Lions career saw him plunder 44 goals in 57 games and he remains the all-time top goalscorer in the English top flight, with 357 strikes shared between Chelsea, Spurs and West Ham. Greaves moved into broadcasting after hanging up his boots, notably presenting the iconic *Saint and Greavsie* show alongside Ian St John.

SEPTEMBER 20

Francis Lee was a big player for Manchester City, scoring 112 league goals in nearly eight years at Maine Road so he was a little miffed when the club sold him to Derby County for £100,000 in 1974. On this day in 1975 Lee scored a superb strike for Derby against his old club at Maine Road. The goal prompted some famous commentary from Barry Davies: 'Lee. Interesting … VERY interesting! Oh! Look at his face! Just look at his face!'

It was Brian Clough who led Derby to their first league title. The great man passed away on this day in 2004 at the age of 69. The man who claimed: 'I certainly wouldn't say I'm the best manager in the business, but I'm in the top one,' could point to results to back up his boast as he won league titles with both Derby County and Nottingham Forest and led the latter to two European Cup triumphs.

SEPTEMBER 21

Today in 1949 the England team lost a home international match to the Republic of Ireland at Everton's Goodison Park ground – it was the first home defeat for England by a visiting team from outside the UK. England were captained by Wolves legend Billy Wright but he could not prevent a 2-0 reverse to the Irish with goals from Con Martin and Peter Farrell.

The Three Lions were again making more of a whimper than a roar on this day in 1983 when they lost 1-0 to Denmark at Wembley in a qualification game for Euro 1984. On the day that Phil Neal won his 50th and final cap, a penalty from Allan Simonsen was enough to win the match for the Danes. The result was another nail in the coffin of England's doomed campaign which ended in them missing out on the tournament in France.

SEPTEMBER 22

Today in 1993 the French champions Olympique Marseille were stripped of their league title after the actions of their chairman came to light. Earlier in 1993 when Marseille were looking forward to meeting Milan in the European Cup final in Munich, the chairman Bernard Tapie didn't want to risk a number of first-team players against the lowly Valenciennes so he bribed them to let Marseille win and make sure none of their players were injured. It worked and the club won the league and the European Cup, but Tapie was found out and as well as losing their league title they were banned from defending their European Cup crown and Tapie was jailed.

On the same day a young Robbie Fowler made his Liverpool debut in their Coca-Cola Cup tie with Fulham at Craven Cottage which the Reds won 3-1. Fowler scored all five goals in the second leg at Anfield two weeks later and was an instant hero with the Kop.

SEPTEMBER 23

In the mid 1980s Liverpool were still at the peak of their powers as Kenny Dalglish continued the amazing run of success the club had been on since the early 1960s. Fulham however were still in their pre-Al Fayed days and had been relegated to the Third Division the season before the two sides were drawn together in the League Cup on this day in 1986. The Reds hammered the Cottagers 10-0 in the first leg. A more respectable 3-2 loss in the second leg did not stop this being the record defeat in the competition.

Also on this day, in 1989 Manchester City were thrashing their cross-town rivals Manchester United in a match still talked about by City fans today. With Alex Ferguson under pressure to win something, the 5-1 scoreline in the Manchester derby did not help his popularity with the Old Trafford faithful.

SEPTEMBER 24

It's seen countless cup finals, the world's best players, a host of wonder goals and what Clive Tyldesley will forever describe as 'that wonderful night in Barcelona'– it was today in 1957 that Camp Nou was opened. Back in the 1950s Barcelona had outgrown their Camp de les Corts ground so set about building a new stadium which took three-and-a-half years and 288 million pesetas to complete. The first game played at Camp Nou pitted Barça against Legia Warsaw, and in case it ever comes up in a pub quiz, the first goal was bagged by Eulogio Martínez in a 4-2 win for the Catalan side.

Also on this day in 1998 George Graham made the most unlikely of career moves when he took the manager's job at Tottenham Hotspur. He was the man who had brought success to Arsenal until he was sacked for taking a bung. Two years as Leeds manager helped his rehabilitation but no one expected him to take the reins at Arsenal's biggest rivals.

SEPTEMBER 25

He is the hero of the thousands of players who turn out for non-league sides every week. Ian Wright was playing for Greenwich Borough and working as a plasterer when he was spotted and signed for Crystal Palace at the ripe old age of 22. After six prolific years with the Eagles, George Graham paid a then club record fee of £2.5m to take Wrighty to Arsenal. On this day in 1991 the front man marked his Gunners debut with a goal in a 1-1 draw with Leicester City at Filbert Street.

Wrighty had long since hung up his boots when the club signed Gilberto Silva in 2002, but the Brazilian midfielder did not have to wait long to make his mark. Today in 2002 he scored in Arsenal's first attack in their Champions League match with PSV in Eindhoven. The goal was timed at 20.07 seconds and was the fastest in Champions League history until Roy Makaay scored in 10.2 seconds for Bayern Munich against Real Madrid in 2007.

SEPTEMBER 26

Today in 1964, Franz Beckenbauer made his international debut for West Germany in a 2-1 defeat of Sweden. He went on to become the only man to win the World Cup both as a captain (1974) and manager of the team (1990). He won 102 caps in a glittering career and was the man detailed to mark Bobby Charlton in the 1966 World Cup final. Nicknamed 'Der Kaiser', he is arguably Germany's most famous player ever and is widely credited with inventing the sweeper role.

A more controversial figure was making waves on this day in 1998. Paolo Di Canio, then playing for Sheffield Wednesday, was red carded in a match with Arsenal at Hillsborough. He thought the sending-off was unjust so pushed referee Paul Alcock, who did a very undignified backwards stumble before falling over. Di Canio was banned for 11 matches and left Wednesday soon afterwards for West Ham.

SEPTEMBER 27

Because of parentage or country of birth, some footballers have the choice of more than one nation to play for, but it is usually only a choice of two. Today in 1999 David Johnson was possibly hedging his bets when he was called up to the Wales squad, having already been involved with the Jamaican and English national teams. Born in Jamaica but holding a British passport meant he could play for the Caribbean side or any of the home nations. He later had a spell with the Scotland set up as well, but eventually plumped for Jamaica, having not played a competitive match for any of the other teams.

For 67 days, Sam Allardyce could call himself England manager. But the former Bolton Wanderers boss's lifelong dream ended in ignominy today in 2016, when he left his post by mutual consent after a *Daily Telegraph* investigation that alleged he offered advice on how to 'get around' rules on player transfers, all while drinking what many thought looked like a pint of wine. On the plus side for Big Sam though, he exited the international stage with a unique 100 per cent record, having overseen a 1-0 win over Slovakia in a 2018 World Cup qualifier in his only game in charge.

SEPTEMBER 28

If you know your history, you will know that Anfield was originally the home of Everton FC before the club moved on over a rent dispute. The first match to ever be played at the ground was on this day in 1884 when Everton beat Earlstown 5-0.

Today in 1996 Arsène Wenger was appointed manager of Arsenal. He built on the foundations laid by George Graham and took the club to the next level, not just winning titles and cups aplenty, but doing it in a style that made Arsenal the most aesthetically pleasing side of their generation. All this and Wenger still found time to develop some of the best players in the world such as Thierry Henry, Patrick Vieira and Cesc Fabregas, personally help design the new stadium and go a whole season unbeaten. All with a fraction of the financial outlay of Arsenal's rivals.

SEPTEMBER 29

Chelsea went goal crazy today in 1971 when they hit eight past a shell-shocked Jeunesse Hautcharage team in a European Cup Winners' Cup match. The minnows from Luxembourg had won the Luxembourg Cup the previous season and their reward was an absolute hammering by Chelsea. The second leg was even more painful as Chelsea scored 13 without reply at Stamford Bridge. The 21-0 scoreline remains the largest score ever for an official UEFA match.

A city was in mourning on this day in 1981 when Bill Shankly died aged 68 in Broadgreen Hospital in Liverpool. The legendary manager transformed the club from Second Division also-rans to the best and most successful team in the country and is remembered as the greatest manager the club ever had. A committed socialist, the Labour Party conference stood for a minute's silence when his death was announced.

SEPTEMBER 30

If just going to the matches, buying a programme, and reading about Manchester United in the paper was just not enough for you, the club had the answer on this day in 1997 when the Old Trafford suits announced they were linking up with Granada to bring the fans MUTV, their very own channel. The channel is most notable for something it never actually broadcast, when an explosive interview with then-skipper Roy Keane, who was laying into some of the top players after a 4-1 loss to Middlesbrough, was pulled at the last minute. Roy left the club soon after.

After a blistering start to his career as Leicester City boss in 2000, Peter Taylor was being talked about as a potential future England manager. Today in 2001, little more than one season later, he was sacked with the club in freefall and heading for relegation. Taylor's replacement Dave Bassett couldn't stop the rot and the club finished bottom of the table.

FOOTBALL
On This Day

OCTOBER

OCTOBER 1

Pelé bowed out today in 1977, bringing his blockbusting 21-year career to a close. The world's most famous player had reached the end of a three-year spell at the New York Cosmos, lapping up the razzmatazz of the North American Soccer League. His final game was a friendly against his only other club – Santos – with the Brazilian scoring a 30-yard free kick to end in style. By the end of the game it was pouring with rain, causing a Brazilian newspaper to explain that 'even the sky was crying'.

In 1995 the seagulls had finished following the trawler and Eric Cantona was back following his nine-month ban for attacking a fan kung-fu style. Naturally he returned in style, scoring a goal and setting one up in United's 2-2 draw with Liverpool.

OCTOBER 2

Talent scouts were at the ready in 2005 as Brazil took on Mexico in the under-17 World Cup final in Peru. The boys from Brazil defied their favourites tag by losing 3-0 to the Mexicans, who were led by an inspired performance from Carlos Vela. Where there's world class young footballers Arsene Wenger isn't normally too far behind, so he snapped up the 16-year-old for a cool £2.5m. The other star of the tournament also caught the eye of Premier League scouts, as Manchester United picked up Anderson for the rather more inflated sum of £17m two years later.

There wasn't much South American skill on show at Selhurst Park in 1991 as Wimbledon and Sheffield Wednesday played in front of the lowest top-flight crowd since the Second World War. Just 3,121 saw the Dons beat Wednesday 2-1.

OCTOBER 3

Gus Poyet must have got out of the right side of bed today in 1999 as he took just 27 seconds to find the net for Chelsea against Manchester United. The Uruguayan inspired a 5-0 win over United at Stamford Bridge that day, but it didn't stop the Red Devils winning the title by 18 points that year as Chelsea limped to fifth place.

Even more impressive than the dive Chelsea's league position took that year was Dida's in AC Milan's 2007 match against Celtic. Just after Scott McDonald had scored the winning goal past the Brazilian shot-stopper, a Celtic fan ran on to the pitch and gave Dida a tap on the shoulder. Dida started to chase the jubilant Scot, but then thought he might be able to milk the situation, so clutched his face and hit the deck. No one was fooled and the keeper received a two-game ban.

OCTOBER 4

Peter Taylor, the right-hand man of Brian Clough, died today in 1990 while on holiday in Majorca, aged 62. Taylor worked with Clough at Hartlepool, Derby and Forest and had an uncanny ability to spot talent and potential. The pair's relationship frayed in the early 1980s and they would never speak again. After Taylor's death Clough spoke of his regret, dedicating his 1994 autobiography to him, saying: 'To Peter. Still miss you badly. You once said: "When you get shot of me there won't be as much laughter in your life." You were right.'

Newcastle won their first game of the season in 2003 when they beat Southampton 1-0, thanks to a goal from former Saint Alan Shearer. Bobby Robson's men were having a torrid start to the season and the three points they picked up at St James' were not enough to lift them out of the relegation zone.

OCTOBER 5

Happier days for Newcastle today in 1946 when they equalled the Football League record win by putting 13 unanswered goals past Newport. The Second Division clash equalled the previous record set by Stockport against Halifax.

One of British football's greats came into the world today in 1922 when Jock Stein was born. The legendary Scottish manager grew up playing the game he loved at the weekends and working in the local carpet shop and down the pit during the week, before starting his managerial career at Dunfermline. He would go on to make his name during 13 years in charge of Celtic where he picked up 11 Scottish League titles, ten Scottish Cups, five Scottish League Cups, and most famously the 1967 European Cup. Stein was the first man to lead a British team to European glory, and all with a team in which every player was born within 30 miles of Glasgow.

OCTOBER 6

It was redemption day for David Beckham in 2001 as he fired home an injury-time free kick against Greece to book England's place in the 2002 World Cup and exorcise the demons of his red card against Argentina in 1998. England had been making hard work of dispatching the well-organised Greek side, but Beckham turned in one of the best individual performances in years, covering every blade of grass as he dragged the Three Lions to the fun and games in Japan and South Korea.

Italian football was getting itself in order today in 1929, as Serie A was created following – surprise, surprise – a match-fixing scandal. This was the first time a national league had been played in the country with Ambrosiana, later to become Internazionale, winning the inaugural *Scudetto*.

OCTOBER 7

Two eras came crashing to a halt today in 2000 when Dietmar Hamann scored the last ever goal at the old Wembley Stadium to give Germany a 1-0 win over England in a World Cup qualifier. Kevin Keegan obviously didn't 'love it', as he headed straight for the toilets where he handed in his resignation in trademark dramatic fashion. As honest as he was emotional, KK admitted that he just didn't have what it took to lead England and saw no point in carrying on.

Over in Germany, officials were getting in a tizzy over former Liverpool striker Sean Dundee's late, late goal. The Karlsruhe striker's shot was adjudged to have crossed the line just after the referee had blown for full-time to earn a 2-2 draw against 1860 Munich, but following protests, the German Football Association ordered the Bundesliga clash to be replayed.

OCTOBER 8

England's under-21 European Championship qualifier against Poland in 1996 was delayed by two hours following a bomb scare. The army were called in to carry out a controlled explosion at Molineux after an over-eager steward mistook a foil-wrapped sandwich for something far more sinister. The subsequent England performance proved to be less than explosive when they drew 0-0, with Riccardo Scimeca missing a penalty. Following Gareth Southgate's miss earlier that summer, it proves you shouldn't let Aston Villa defenders anywhere near the opposition penalty spot.

These days the same should be said about Dave Bassett and the dugout. In 2001 Bassett was given the top job at Leicester City, where he would remain for only six months before his assistant Micky Adams took over with the Foxes teetering on the brink of relegation. Bassett was moved upstairs to a director of football role, and apart from a caretaker spell at Southampton has not got his hands dirty since.

OCTOBER 9

One of the finest goalscorers England has ever produced passed away today in 1988, as Jackie Milburn died at the age of 64. His war-interrupted 14-year spell at Newcastle United saw him find the net 200 times, a record which stood until fellow local lad Alan Shearer broke it in 2006. His funeral saw 30,000 admirers pay their respects and the club honoured him with a pair of statues and named their new stand after him.

David Beckham was on the end of another controversial carding today in 2004 when he received a yellow for a foul on Wales defender Ben Thatcher. A storm brewed up when Beckham boasted that the foul was deliberate, as it earned him a suspension for a game he knew he would miss though injury anyway. Mr Posh Spice boasted: 'It was deliberate. I am sure some people think that I have not got the brains to be clever, but I do have the brains.'

OCTOBER 10

As CV's go it wasn't too bad: the last Englishman to win the title, the only man to have had two spells as England manager and the former FA technical director. But when Sunderland appointed Howard Wilkinson as their replacement for Peter Reid today in 2002 there was a distinct lack for enthusiasm from the fans at the Stadium of Light. Twenty games and two wins later their scepticism was proved right, as Sergeant Wilko was disposed of and the Black Cats hurtled towards relegation with a then-record low of 19 points.

Similarly poor football was on display at Wembley in 1999, as England put in a dismal performance against Bulgaria, drawing 0-0 in their Euro 2000 qualifier. Manager Glenn Hoddle was not impressed, but still found time to talk his usual nonsense: 'A 0-0 draw is sometimes worse than a 1-1 draw.'

GEORGE WEAH IS SEEN HERE PLAYING HIS LAST INTERNATIONAL MATCH FOR LIBERIA. HE RAN FOR PRESIDENT OF HIS COUNTRY BUT LOST IN OCTOBER 2005 (SEE OVER).

OCTOBER 11

Back in the good ol' days when a player retired he would buy a local pub and spend his days propping up the bar and telling his punters about his past glories. Former World Player of the Year George Weah had loftier ambitions though, as he ran for president in his native Liberia today in 2005. Weah eventually lost to Ellen Johnson-Sirleaf in a run-off, but remained in politics and won the 2017 election.

Somewhat less diplomatic than Weah, Paul Gascoigne had to offer a grovelling apology to the nation of Norway today in 1992. When asked by a Norwegian camera crew if he had a message for England's upcoming opponents he responded with: 'Yes. F**k off Norway.' He then ran away laughing.

OCTOBER 12

In 1993 the man who won the World Cup for England died. Geoff Hurst? Bobby Moore? Sir Alf? No, it was Tofik Bakhramov, or 'the Russian linesman' who has gone down in history as the man who awarded England's controversial third goal in the 1966 World Cup final. 'Russian linesman' was a misnomer as Bakhramov was actually from Azerbaijan and has even had the national stadium in capital Baku named after him. (If you're reading this Graham Poll, don't get any ideas – Wembley already has a name.)

Without Tofik England would never have had the constant pressure of '1966 and all that' as a reason why they fail to win anything. In 1999 the scene was set for the next England failure as UEFA announced that Portugal would host Euro 2004 ahead of the much-fancied Spanish bid.

OCTOBER 13

One of football's greatest derbies was played out for the first time today in 1894 as Liverpool and Everton met for the first time. In a city that is truly obsessed with football 'the friendly derby' polarises friends, families, colleagues and lovers across Merseyside like nothing else. Everton drew first blood as they beat the Reds 3-0 at Goodison Park, two years after they had moved out of Anfield following a rent dispute.

Although it seems like he's been around since the 1890s, it was only today in 1993 that Swedish striker Henrik Larsson made his international debut against fellow Scandinavians Finland. The former Celtic and Barcelona striker turned out for his country 93 times, scoring 36 goals during an international career that saw more comebacks than Rocky Balboa after he came out of retirement in 2004 and 2008 to spearhead his country's European Championship campaigns.

OCTOBER 14

Mark Bosnich was hauled before the FA today in 1996 when he showed that his comic timing was as bad as his ability to 'just say no' when he performed a Nazi salute at White Hart Lane in front of 40,000 baying Spurs fans – many of them Jewish. The Aston Villa keeper claimed it was a joke directed at Jürgen Klinsmann, who had actually left the club a year earlier. The real joke ended up being the paltry £1,000 fine that the FA gave him, as they obviously bought into the Aussie's 'it's political correctness gone mad' defence.

England's laboured attempts to qualify for Euro 2000 continued today in 1998 as they struggled to a 3-0 win over part-timers Luxembourg. A late Gareth Southgate goal added some gloss to the score after the minnows had missed a fifth-minute penalty. It was about this time that the 'there's no easy games in international football any more' cliché really started to pick up steam.

OCTOBER 15

In 1973 Derby chairman Sam Longson made one of those decisions that rocks a club to its foundations. Brian Clough, the man who had delivered the league title to the Baseball Ground for the first time ever was sacked 12 games into the season. Longson and the board were growing tired of Ol' Big 'Ead's outspoken nature, particularly after he called Juventus 'cheating bastards' following their loss to the Italian side in the European Cup semi-finals the previous season. After short but not always sweet spells at Brighton and Leeds he joined Derby's bitter rivals Nottingham Forest who twice became champions of Europe under Clough.

Preston got their name in the history books today in 1887 when they set an English goalscoring record by beating Hyde United 26-0 in a first round FA Cup tie. Jimmy Ross inspired the Hyde-ing by putting seven past the Tigers.

OCTOBER 16

England played their first ever game in Southampton today in 2002 as they took on Macedonia at St Mary's, but the same old failings were still in evidence. Fresh from his error against Brazil in the 2002 World Cup, David Seaman saw Artim Šakiri score directly from a corner, as England limped to a 2-2 draw with the side ranked 90th in the world. Alan Smith rounded off a poor night for the Three Lions when he was sent off in the dying minutes after a horribly mistimed tackle.

Showing a bit more backbone were Liverpool in 2001, as they beat Dynamo Kiev 2-1 in the Champions League days after Gérard Houllier was rushed to hospital during half-time of a Premier League match against Leeds United. Houllier had suffered a dissected aorta and underwent an eleven-hour operation. He was back in the dugout five months later.

OCTOBER 17

Seven years earlier, Sir Alf and his England side had been the toast of the nation, having reached football nirvana in the 1966 World Cup final. But today in 1973 was a different story, as England fell short in their attempts to qualify for the 1974 World Cup when Poland held them to a 1-1 draw at Wembley. The Polish hero that night was goalkeeper Jan Tomaszewski, who Brian Clough had labelled a 'clown' in the build up to the game. Needless to say, the tears weren't his that night.

Showing a precedent that their successors Leeds United would one day live up to, Leeds City auctioned off their playing staff and other assets of the club today in 1919 following their dissolution for financial irregularities. The auction at the Metropole Hotel in Leeds saw 16 members of the side bought by nine different clubs for a total of £9,250.

OCTOBER 18

Fulham fans were mourning the death of their greatest ever player when Johnny Haynes died today in 2005 following a road accident. A one-club man, Haynes racked up 658 appearances for the club and was famed for being their first player to earn £100 a week after the £20 wage cap was abolished. Chuck in a Brylcreem sponsorship deal and you have a man who was well ahead of his time.

One player who probably won't be as fondly remembered is Frank Leboeuf. Today in 1999 the sulky Frenchman was speaking at Oxford University Union and had beef with David Beckham (who he described as 'arrogant') and Karl-Heinz Riedle (who he called a 'cheat'.) Towards the end of his career he was voted the French league's most overrated and arrogant player by his fellow professionals, in a poll only the French could come up with.

OCTOBER 19

Norwich City pulled off the greatest upset in their history in 1993 as they became the only ever English side to defeat Bayern Munich in their Olympic Stadium. Playing in Europe for the first time after finishing third in the debut Premier League season, goals from Jeremy Goss and Mark Bowen gave the Canaries a 2-1 lead to take into the second leg of their UEFA Cup tie. A 1-1 draw at Carrow Road ensured that Norwich progressed in one of English football's greatest European upsets.

In 2002 English football was anointing it's next messiah, as 16-year-old Wayne Rooney scored a belter for Everton against Arsenal to become the Premier League's youngest ever scorer. In his textbook over-excited manner Clive Tyldesley commanded us to: 'Remember the name: Wayne Rooney!' and the hype began.

OCTOBER 20

There were handbags at Old Trafford today in 1990 as Arsenal and Manchester United got stuck into each other. Unlike most 'fights' you see on the football pitch, there were a fair few kicks and punches flying around after Anders Limpar and Denis Irwin initially squared up. A 21-man brawl ensued, with David Seaman being the only man on the field to sit out the fracas. (Presumably he was worried about having his hair pulled or didn't want to leave his line in case Nayim was knocking around.) The FA took a dim view of events, fining both clubs £50,000 and deducting Arsenal two points and United one.

United were having another bad day in 1996 as they suffered their biggest defeat for 12 years when Newcastle beat them 5-0. Kevin Keegan's only complaint that night was that 'the league won't give us more than three points for it!'

OCTOBER 21

As England searched for Kevin Keegan's replacement in 2000 they were finding the same scarcity of candidates as there usually is when the job comes up. FA chief exec Adam Crozier decided that to buy a bit of time he'd call on a temp, and made an official approach to Newcastle to employ Bobby Robson today in 2000, but Freddy Shepherd refused to play ball and wouldn't let Uncle Bobby return to the national team. Crozier eventually appointed Sven-Göran Eriksson.

When Paul Ince was summoned by the FA today in 1998 it wasn't to wish him a happy 31st birthday, but to charge him with misconduct for flashing a V-sign after being sent off in England's opening Euro 2000 qualifier against Sweden. The birthday boy had earlier received a three-match ban from UEFA.

OCTOBER 22

The career of England's greatest ever goalkeeper was prematurely ended today in 1972 when Gordon Banks lost the sight in his right eye following a car crash. Banks had been driving home for a session with the Stoke physiotherapist when his car ended up in a ditch after he lost control. Banks attempted to play on, but the loss of binocular vision meant he had no hope of pulling off saves like his legendary stop from Pelé in the 1970 World Cup.

A poll at the end of the 20th century ranked Banks as the second best, behind only the Russian goalie Lev Yashin who was born today in 1929. 'The Black Spider' as he was known compiled some outrageously good statistics during his career, achieving 270 clean sheets in 812 games. He was also deeply patriotic, claiming that 'the joy of seeing Yuri Gagarin flying in space is only superseded by the joy of a good penalty save.'

OCTOBER 23

Wembley Stadium played host to the stars today in 1963 as Sir Alf Ramsey's England team took on a Rest of the World XI to celebrate the 100th anniversary of the FA. The bulk of Sir Alf's 1966 side took on the likes of Di Stéfano, Puskás, Eusébio and Denis Law. The 100,000 in attendance went home happy as England won 2-1, and plenty of backslapping ensued amongst the suits at the FA.

Today in 1999 Arsenal striker Kanu left it late, scoring a last-gasp hat-trick as the Gunners came back from 2-0 down to Chelsea with 15 minutes remaining. The Nigerian went on to be named African Footballer of the Year as Arsenal got over the loss of Nicolas Anelka and gave headline writers the chance to splash puns such as 'Kanu believe it' across the tabloids.

OCTOBER 24

When your team's nickname is simply 'The Club', you've got to have a bit of history to back it up. And history is one thing that Sheffield FC has more of than anyone else, as they are the world's oldest football club. Established today in 1857, Nathaniel Creswick and William Prest founded the club that has been recognised by FIFA as the oldest in the world, joining Real Madrid as the only two teams to have been awarded the FIFA Order of Merit.

Staying in Yorkshire, David O'Leary's young Leeds United side took on Barcelona at Elland Road today in 2000 after being battered at Camp Nou in their first group game. Thanks largely to an outstanding performance from 23-year-old goalkeeper Paul Robinson, playing because of an injury to Nigel Martyn, Leeds held Barça to a 1-1 draw and progressed at their expense.

OCTOBER 25

Football has managed to upset a lot of people over the years – it has even been the cause of wars – but today in 2000 the beautiful game took on an opponent that it couldn't overcome: Cilla Black. ITV had recently won the rights for the Premier League highlights and started the season showing their version of *Match of the Day* at 7pm on a Saturday night, ousting *Blind Date*. After only a couple of months though, the ratings failed to match those of Cilla and 'our Graham', so ITV bosses shifted the football back to 10.30pm as Cilla gave the beautiful game a pounding.

Back on the pitch, in 1989 Frankie Bunn had his day in the spotlight when the Oldham striker scored six goals against Scarborough to set a League Cup individual scoring record.

OCTOBER 26

It all sounds so Dickensian: a cold, autumn night in Victorian London at the Freemason's Tavern in Great Queen Street, with our protagonist Ebenezer Cobb Morley. But this isn't the start of *Great Expectations* or *Oliver Twist*, but the beginning of the Football Association. It was today in 1863 that eleven clubs and schools, led by Morley, met for the first time to create a standardised set of rules for clubs across the country to follow.

Howard Wilkinson's Leeds United side returned to the top of the league for the first time since the days of Don Revie today in 1991 when a Brian Kilcline own goal gave them a 1-0 win over Oldham. In the final season before the Premier League was formed Leeds finished top of the pile, as Wilkinson became the last English manager to win the title.

OCTOBER 27

Glenn Hoddle celebrates another year of not being punished for his sins in a previous life today, as the former England manager was born on this day in 1957. Before he became a promising young manager, then a mediocre middle-aged manager, and now an unemployed old manager, young Glenn was pretty nifty on the pitch. As a player he gave Spurs fans 12 years of midfield genius before hooking up with Arsene Wenger at Monaco.

Leicester City were in mourning today in 2018, when their owner Vichai Srivaddhanaprabha was among five people to die when his helicopter crashed outside the club's stadium following a match against West Ham. The 60-year-old had purchased the Foxes in 2010 and it was under his stewardship that the club completed their stunning Premier League title campaign in 2016.

OCTOBER 28

It may well be football hearsay to claim that Pelé wasn't the best Brazilian to ever play the game, but the bow-legged legend Garrincha, who was born today in 1933, is considered by many back in Brazil to be the best of the bunch. Soon after he was born with a left leg that curved outwards and a right one that bent inwards, stories circulated about a boy 'who lived in the wood with bent legs who could dribble like the devil'.

Neil Ruddock managed to bring out the devil in quite a few of his opponents, with Patrick Vieira being one of them after he was banned today in 1999 for spitting at the man known as 'Razor'. In addition to a four-match ban and £30,000 fine, the Frenchman was also disciplined for confronting a police officer after his red card at Upton Park, getting a further two-match ban and having to cough up another £15,000.

OCTOBER 29

Adrian Mutu was given a punishment that wasn't to be sniffed at today in 2004 when he was sacked by Chelsea after testing positive for cocaine. The Blues ditched their £15.8m Romanian striker who claimed that he had used the drug in order to improve his sex life, amongst claims that he had lived up to every Transylvanian stereotype in the book by sucking on the blood of his partner.

None of those sort of shenanigans at Old Trafford a year later though, as Fergie's men became the first side to score 1,000 goals since the start of the Premiership in 1992. You'd have done well to raise a smile on Sir Alex's face though, as Cristiano Ronaldo's injury-time goal proved to be only a consolation as Middlesbrough cruised to a 4-1 win.

OCTOBER 30

After a career that saw him rise from the shanty town of Villa Fiorito to lifting the World Cup and being hailed by many as the greatest player of all time, Diego Armando Maradona hung up his boots today in 1997, on his 37th birthday. Maradona bowed out just the way he would have wanted to, leading Boca Juniors to a 2-1 victory over their bitter rivals River Plate.

A record that is unlikely ever to be broken was set today in 1937 when 68,029 fans turned up for Aston Villa's Second Division clash with Coventry City. Villa would go on to win the division that season, with the Sky Blues just missing out on promotion in fourth place.

OCTOBER 31

Today in 2002 there was a Halloween horror show from Madagascan side Stade Olympique L'Emyrne who lost to AS Adema by a world record score of 149-0. Clocking in at the rate of almost two goals every minute, SOE deliberately fired the ball into their own goal time and time again in protest over a refereeing decision that saw their coach Ratsimandresy Ratsarazaka lose his rag with the officials. This record win ended an eventful week for Adema who had just clinched the Malagasy title.

It took Ruud van Nistelrooy almost 200 games to score that many goals during his spell at Manchester United, but today in 1998 he bagged his first ever hat-trick, when he scored a treble for PSV against Sparta. Young Ruud made his international debut three weeks later and would end the season as the top scorer in the Eredivisie.

FOOTBALL
On This Day

NOVEMBER

NOVEMBER 1

The suits down at White Hart Lane seem to have something of a penchant for employing former star players as managers in their increasingly desperate efforts to win something. In some cases like Bill Nicholson and Keith Burkinshaw it has proved highly successful. In others, like Glenn Hoddle and Ossie Ardiles, things have not quite worked out and it was on this day in 1994 that Ossie was summoned to then Spurs' chairman Alan Sugar's home and told, in the style that has since become familiar to millions: 'You're fired.'

Three years to the day later and more managerial merry-go-round antics were afoot in Portugal when the mustachioed Graeme Souness was installed as the new manager of Benfica following the appointment of João Vale e Azevedo as club president. Souness was given a two-and-a-half year contract which, according to Azevedo, was subject to 'the attainment of objectives'. Clearly they were not attained and Souness was sacked two years later without winning anything.

NOVEMBER 2

Arsenal manager Terry Neill paid Wolves £220,000 to bring striker Alan Sunderland to Highbury today in 1977. It was to prove an astute bit of business, especially in the FA Cup final of 1979 when he scored the winner in the famous 'five-minute final'.

Manchester United captain Roy Keane was on the comeback trail today in 2002 when his ban for his X-rated challenge on Alf-Inge Haaland ended. The FA had to act after Keane's autobiography was published. The offending passage read: 'I'd waited long enough. I f***ing hit him hard. The ball was there (I think). Take that you c***. And don't ever stand over me sneering about fake injuries.'

November 3

After playing a key role in the heady success at Manchester United through the 1990s first as a coach and then assistant manager, Brian Kidd was beginning to tire of being the monkey to Ferguson's organ grinder and started to think he might make a pretty good gaffer himself. He went to prove himself at Blackburn Rovers but soon found it was tough at the top as Rovers were relegated, having won the Premiership just four years earlier. Today in 1999 Kidd was sacked with the club lurching dangerously towards another relegation.

Boston manager Steve Evans was also in trouble today in 2006 when he, along with club chairman Patrick Malkinson, were given suspended sentences at Southwark Crown Court for their creative tax accounting. Their scam saved the club £323,000 in taxes which allowed them to attract more expensive players than their competitors, and achieve two promotions to the Football League.

November 4

Today in 1945 at Croydon airport an aeroplane touched down with Dynamo Moscow on board – the first Soviet club to visit the UK. The English press was quick to dismiss the Muscovites' chances with one paper warning fans 'not to expect much from this bunch of factory workers.' Dynamo were not listening though as they drew 3-3 with Chelsea, demolished Cardiff 10-0, drew 2-2 with Rangers and beat an Arsenal side containing Stanley Matthews 4-3 at Highbury. Matthews bigged-up Dynamo as 'the finest team ever to visit these islands – we have certainly learned a thing or two from these Dynamos.'

On this day in 2001 Pep Guardiola failed a drugs test after his Brescia team's match with Lazio. It was the second time he had tested positive for nandrolone but the Spain midfielder vehemently protested his innocence and threatened to quit football unless he could prove he was not guilty. He was banned for four months but appealed against the decision and was cleared of any wrongdoing in October 2007.

NOVEMBER 5

Herbert Chapman was the Arsene Wenger of his day. In his ten years as manager of Arsenal he took what modern-day management gurus would term 'a global approach' to the running of the club and immersed himself in every detail. Not only was he a revolutionary coach but he was also behind many developments in the game including numbers on players' shirts and games under floodlights. He was behind the white sleeves of the Gunners' strip and on this day in 1932 he persuaded London Electric Railway to rename Gillespie Road Underground station after the club. Arsenal station is the only one to be named after a football club.

Before taking over at Arsenal Chapman had won the league two years in a row with Huddersfield Town. Another former Huddersfield boss is Bill Shankly, who was appointed on this day in 1956. Shanks could not repeat Chapman's success and failed to get the club promoted from the Second Division.

NOVEMBER 6

Today in 1986 the Manchester United board made a move that would have a huge impact on the club and English football in general when they appointed Alex Ferguson as their new manager. Despite a bit of a rocky start which nearly saw Fergie sacked, he led the club to FA Cup success in 1990. Once he started winning things he couldn't stop and hoovered up trophies until his retirement in 2013.

Another managerial appointment also took place on this day in 2001 although it was not quite the cataclysmic moment in football history that Ferguson's appointment was. Former England midfielder Carlton Palmer was handed the reins at Stockport County. One relegation and two years later Carlton was sacked.

NOVEMBER 7

More managerial merry-go-round action today in 1990 when Howard Kendall left Manchester City to take the reins at Everton for a second time. During the 1980s Kendall had masterminded the most successful period in the club's history but he left to manage in Spain with his assistant Colin Harvey taking over as Everton boss. Things did not go so well for Harvey and he was sacked in 1990. He was not out of work for long though as Kendall immediately brought him back to the club as his assistant.

One for the geographers today in 2015, as the Premier League served up a unique cartographic oddity. Newly promoted Bournemouth began the season as the most southerly side ever to play in the competition and today hosted Newcastle United, the most northerly side. And as luck would have it, Carrow Road played host to the most eastern and western sides to ever make it to the Premier League, as Norwich City took on Swansea City. In a blow to south-west enthusiasts, the Magpies and the Canaries would both win 1-0.

NOVEMBER 8

Today in 1975 German referee Wolf-Dieter Ahlenfelder joined the likes of Paul Merson and Paul McGrath by taking to the pitch a little the worse for wear to officiate the match between Werder Bremen and Hannover 96. When he blew for half-time with just 29 minutes played it was obvious something was amiss. His linesman corrected him and the game continued. Afterwards he said: 'We are men – we don't drink Fanta.'

Steve Coppell liked a drink or two as well; he once said he could not remember exactly why he liked Kevin Doyle after seeing him play in Ireland. He said: 'I had five pints of Guinness in the afternoon and it was all a bit blurred.' Today in 1996 Coppell quit his job as Manchester City manager after just 33 days, citing stress and the pressures of the job as his reason for his shock decision.

NOVEMBER 9

Every team loves to beat Manchester United but none more so than their cross-city rivals Manchester City. The blue team tasted sweet victory over their more successful red counterparts today in 2002 in the last ever Manchester derby at Maine Road. They used to chant 'feed the Goat and he will score' but it was the unlikely source of Gary Neville who fed Shaun Goater when his poor back pass to Fabien Barthez let Goater in to score City's second in a 3-1 win.

Former Manchester United captain Bryan Robson was unveiled as West Bromwich Albion manager on this day in 2005, taking over from Gary Megson with the team 17th in the Premiership. By Christmas the team was rock bottom of the league and dead certs for relegation but Robson oversaw an impressive late season surge. It culminated in a dramatic last gasp escape on the final day of the season when they beat Portsmouth at the Hawthorns to keep their top-flight place.

NOVEMBER 10

'But then one night in Ro-ome we were strong, we had grown.' So sang Baddiel and Skinner in their 1998 World Cup version of 'Three Lions'. The duo were referring to the match today in 1997 in which England needed a draw away to Italy to qualify for the 1998 World Cup. Paul Gascoigne played superbly and Paul Ince did his Terry Butcher impression, playing with a bloodstained shirt, as England held on for the 0-0 draw they needed.

For a ticket to the 2002 World Cup the Republic of Ireland had to beat Iran in a two-legged play-off. The Irish hosted their opponents at Lansdowne Road today in 2001 with a goal each from Ian Harte and Robbie Keane giving them a 2-0 lead. In the second leg Shay Given played a blinder to keep the score 1-0 to Iran and give the Irish a 2-1 aggregate win and a place in the finals.

NOVEMBER 11

Today in 2006 was the Mike Newell show. The former Luton Town boss was incensed by female assistant referee Amy Rayner's decision not to award his team a penalty. He said: 'She shouldn't be here. I know that sounds sexist but I am sexist. It is tokenism for the politically-correct idiots. We have a problem in this country with political correctness and bringing women into the game is not the way to improve refereeing and officialdom. It is absolutely beyond belief. It is bad enough with the incapable referees and linesmen we have but if you start bringing in women, you have big problems.'

Chris Coleman turned up 90 minutes late for a press conference today in 2007 when he was Real Sociedad boss. He told the gathered hacks that he was late because his washing machine had flooded his flat. The club were not so sure and two days later Cookie had to come clean that he had actually been out partying until 5am at a student disco the night before.

NOVEMBER 12

Some double acts are just meant to be. John and Paul, Barry and Paul Chuckle and Simon and Garfunkel were all duos that clicked together perfectly but today saw the demise of a partnership that was doomed from the off. It was on this day in 1998 that Liverpool's joint manager Roy Evans was given the boot from the boot room, to leave Gérard Houllier in sole charge of the team.

Manchester United's best ever goalkeeper Peter Schmeichel told the world he would be leaving Old Trafford at the end of the season today in 1998. He said: 'I have had a fantastic career with United and I owe it to the club, players, and fans to do everything I can to finish on a successful note.' That he did in emphatic style, winning the European Cup in his final game as the club won their historic treble.

NOVEMBER 13

On this day in 1999 the auldest of auld enemies met at Hampden Park in the first leg of a Euro 2000 play-off which Keegan's England won 2-0. The Scots managed a 1-0 win in the second leg at Wembley but England were through. After the match Keegan was at his eternally optimistic best about the tournament. 'I know you'll laugh,' he said after the lacklustre display, 'but we have a chance to win it.' If only Kev, if only.

A landmark deal in football history occurred today in 2007 when fan website MyFootballClub agreed a takeover of Blue Square Premier team Ebbsfleet United. The 20,000 members of the website each paid £35 to provide the £700,000 needed to buy a 51 per cent stake in the club. Each member was given an equal vote on running the club including transfers and team selections.

NOVEMBER 14

World Cup winners Italy arrived at Highbury to play England in a friendly match today in 1934. Keen to put the arrogant English in their place, and spurred on by the promise of a new Alfa Romeo from Mussolini if they won, the Italians were fired up. However, they lost defender Luis Monti to injury and in those pre-substitute days the Azzuri were soon 3-0 down to an England team containing seven Arsenal players. Losing and wounded, the Italians turned the match into the nastiest friendly ever played, lashing out at their opponents and inflicting cuts, bruises and broken arms and noses as they clawed two goals back. The Italians returned home as heroes but the English belief in their superiority was unshaken. *The Times* reported: 'On paper it looks as though the Italians were unfortunate to lose. Actually they were not.'

Another fiercely contested match had to be delayed when a fox ran on to the pitch today in 1996 at Parkhead during an Old Firm game. The fox evaded several Celtic and Rangers players before dashing back into the crowd.

NOVEMBER 15

Today marks the senior debut of perhaps the greatest player Europe has ever produced. A 17-year-old Johan Cruyff first crossed the white line on this day in 1964 when his Ajax side took on GVAV. They lost 3-1 that day but the Ajax faithful had a glimpse of the future as Cruyff scored their consolation goal. The following season he scored 25 times as Ajax won the league. Cruyff was the genius around which Rinus Michels built his revolutionary Total Football philosophy as Ajax won 14 trophies in seven years.

Kevin Keegan never had the sublime skill that Cruyff possessed but he made the most of what he did have to become a leading figure for both club and country. The only Englishman to have been named European Footballer of the Year twice, it was today in 1972 that Keegan made his England debut in a World Cup qualifier against Wales at Ninian Park which England won 1-0. KK scored his first England goal six months later and went on to become England captain.

NOVEMBER 16

Tottenham striker Willie Hall set a record on this day in 1938 when he scored a hat-trick in three minutes and thirty seconds for England against Northern Ireland. He scored five overall in the match – a 7-0 win for England. At the time Hall's hat-trick was the fastest ever in international football and his record stood for 62 years until Japanese striker Masashi Nakayama beat his record by 27 seconds in a match against Brunei in 2000.

A pretty handy goalscorer himself in his time, these days Gary Lineker is the perma-tanned, crisp-hawking foil to the likes of Alan Shearer and Ian Wright on *Match of the Day*. Today in 2005 he proved he was more than just a one-trick pony when he was unveiled by the BBC as their new golf presenter.

NOVEMBER 17

England went to San Marino on this day in 1993 needing to win by seven clear goals and hope Holland lost to make it to the 1994 World Cup. Graham Taylor certainly did not like it when the tiny minnows, with a population about equal to the capacity of Bolton's Reebok Stadium, scored with barely eight seconds on the clock after a misplaced Stuart Pearce back pass. England eventually won 7-1, but they didn't qualify and Taylor resigned six days later.

Ugly scenes of racist chanting marred another England match today in 2004 when the Three Lions played Spain in a friendly at the Bernabéu. Spain won 1-0 thanks to an Asier Del Horno goal but in an ill-tempered game Ashley Cole and Shaun Wright-Phillips were subjected to racist chanting from the crowd. FIFA fined the Spanish Football Federation £44,750 for the abuse.

NOVEMBER 18

Today in 2005 Roy Keane made his shock exit from Manchester United after rumours of a fall out with Sir Alex Ferguson. Keane had been stirring things up for a while at United, firstly by dismissing a pre-season trip to Portugal as a waste of time and then giving an interview to MUTV that was never broadcast which laid into several of his teammates. Aiming his wrath at Rio Ferdinand, Keane said: 'Just because you are paid £120,000-a-week and play well for 20 minutes against Tottenham, you think you are a superstar.' Despite once being his most trusted player, Keane had become a loose cannon and Ferguson acted in a typically ruthless manner to rid himself of his troublesome captain.

One year after Keane's departure Manchester United were looking to the future when Freddy Adu, the most hyped young player in the world, arrived at Old Trafford for a trial with the club. The young forward was still only 17 when he pitched up at United but the trial came to nothing and he signed for Benfica in July 2007.

DID HE NOT LIKE THAT. ENGLAND BOSS GRAHAM TAYLOR WAS FORCED OUT OF THE JOB IN NOVEMBER 1993.

November 19

Pelé made history today in 1969 when he scored the 1,000th goal of his career. The Brazilian master scored the record-breaking goal in his 909th match at the age of just 29. After he scored the penalty for Santos against Vasco da Gama many of the 80,000 fans packed inside the Maracanã stadium mobbed him and the Vasco goalkeeper took off his jersey to reveal a congratulatory message written on a t-shirt underneath. Pelé's final goal tally is also a matter of some dispute but FIFA reckon he hit 1,281 goals in 1,363 games.

Meanwhile today in 1997 Paul Gascoigne was getting himself into trouble again when he was red carded in an Old Firm match at Parkhead. It was the first time he had been sent off for Rangers but even the man he fouled, Celtic's Morten Wieghorst, thought it was a bit harsh.

November 20

Bournemouth legend Ted MacDougal set an FA Cup record on this day in 1971 when he netted nine times in a first round tie against non-league Margate. SuperMac scored five in the first half and another four after the interval in an 11-0 win. It remains the most goals scored by one player in an FA Cup match.

The most controversial World Cup of modern times began today in 2022. From FIFA's initial decision to award the tournament to Qatar to the upending of the football calendar, via the use of low-paid migrant labour to build stadia and infrastructure plus the accusations that the state was looking to 'sportswash' its human rights abuses, FIFA had created a deafening cacophony of pre-tournament noise. In this opening match, the hosts went down 2-0 to Ecuador at the Al Bayt Stadium in Al Khor.

NOVEMBER 21

When Robert Pires and Thierry Henry attempted their ill-fated two-man penalty at Highbury against Manchester City in 2005 they were trying to emulate Johan Cruyff and Jesper Olsen when they pulled off the feat in 1982. It was on this day in 1964, nearly 20 years before Cruyff, that Mike Trebilcock scored from a pass from his Plymouth Argyle teammate Johnny Newman direct from a penalty kick. Oddly enough, just as they would 41 years later against Arsenal's Pires and Henry, Man City provided the opposition for Argyle that day.

Perhaps even more farcical than Pires' penalty attempt was England's performance today in 2007 when, under the guidance of Steve McClaren, the team conspired to lose 3-2 at Wembley to the Croatia team who had already qualified for Euro 2008, ensuring England would not be going to the finals.

NOVEMBER 22

There were extraordinary scenes on this day in 1995 when in the middle of Blackburn's Champions League away tie at Spartak Moscow, Rovers team-mates David Batty and Graeme Le Saux ended up in a fist-fight. After clattering into one another as they went for the same ball, they traded insults and then blows with Le Saux punching his team-mate. Spartak coach Oleg Romantsev said: 'Before the match I told my players they will be playing against 11 guys ready to fight for each other for 90 minutes – not with each other.'

Crystal Palace's orange chairman Simon Jordan took to the High Court on this day in 2001 to prevent manager Steve Bruce from walking out to take the top job at Birmingham City. Jordan had refused to accept Bruce's resignation but eventually relented. Bruce became Birmingham manager in December with former Blues boss Trevor Francis going the other way. Jordan later said of Birmingham chairman David Gold: 'If I see another David Gold interview on the poor East End Jewish boy done good I'll impale myself on one of his dildos.'

NOVEMBER 23

Perhaps the greatest scam ever was pulled off on this day in 1996 when Ali Dia, easily the worst player to have ever graced the Premier League, made his first, last and only top-flight appearance for Southampton. Legend has it Saints boss Graeme Souness had been called by Dia's agent, who pretended to be George Weah and recommended Dia, who he claimed was his cousin. Souness snapped him up and without seeing him play brought him on to replace Matt Le Tissier in Saints' match with Leeds. After 20 minutes it was clear Dia was hopelessly out of his depth and a red-faced Souness had to haul him off.

David O'Leary took a gamble of a different kind today in 2000 when he spent £18m to take Rio Ferdinand from West Ham to Leeds. At the time it was a record for an English defender but Rio lived up to his price tag and was eventually sold to Manchester United for nearly £30m just two years later.

NOVEMBER 24

Today in 2004 Harry Redknapp quit as manager of Portsmouth FC after two-and-a-half years in charge. Harry was not impressed by the arrival of Velimir Zajec as director of football and resigned. On leaving Fratton Park, Redknapp denied he would take the manager's job at struggling Southampton. 'Go down the road to Southampton? No chance,' he said. Two weeks later he was installed as Saints' new boss with a brief to save them from relegation. He failed.

Milan Mandarić appointed Frenchman Alain Perrin to replace Redknapp but exactly a year to the day after Harry walked out, Perrin was given the sack after winning only four of 20 Premiership games.

NOVEMBER 25

England, self-appointed masters of football, were expecting to thrash Hungary at Wembley on this day in 1953. Instead Ferenc Puskás and his Mighty Magyars dished out the spanking, beating England 6-3. It was the first time England had lost a home match to any team from outside the British Isles. Sir Bobby Robson, who watched the match, said: 'The game had a profound effect, not just on myself but on all of us. That one game alone changed our thinking. We thought we would demolish this team – England at Wembley, we are the masters, they are the pupils. It was absolutely the other way.' There is even a bar in Budapest named the 6:3 Bar in honour of the result.

Two of the game's true mavericks passed away on this date. In 2005, former Manchester United star George Best, who was dubbed 'the fifth Beatle', died after a long battle with alcoholism. Fifteen years later to the day, Argentinian legend Diego Maradona suffered a cardiac arrest and died in his sleep.

NOVEMBER 26

Jan Molby got to keep the match ball today in 1986 when he scored a hat-trick for Liverpool in their 3-1 win over Coventry in the League Cup fourth round replay. Jan was a touch fortunate to take the ball home with him however, as all three of his goals were penalties. Liverpool folklore has it that this was Steven Gerrard's first game at Anfield.

On this day in 1992 a transfer was completed that would have a profound effect on English football. League champions Leeds United sold Eric Cantona to cross-Pennine rivals Manchester United for a paltry £1.2m. The deal tipped the balance of power dramatically as Leeds, riding high at the time, sank down the league while Manchester United went on to win their first league title for 26 years, making Cantona the first player to win back to back titles with two different clubs.

NOVEMBER 27

The world of football was in mourning today in 2011 following the tragic death of Gary Speed at the age of just 42. As a player, Speed was hugely popular among both fans and team-mates during his successful stints at Leeds United, Everton, Newcastle United, Bolton Wanderers and Sheffield United, before moving into management, first with the Blades, then the Wales national team.

Len Shackleton passed away on this day in 2000, aged 78. Shack played for Newcastle before joining Sunderland where his showman tendencies made him a firm favourite. During one match with Arsenal, Shack's team were 2-1 up with five minutes left. He dribbled the ball into the Gunners' penalty area before standing on the ball and pretending to comb his hair while looking at his watch as the remaining minutes ticked down. In 1956 he released his autobiography and used his nickname as the title: *The Clown Prince of Football*. It famously contained a chapter entitled: 'The Average Director's Knowledge of Football'. Underneath the title was a completely blank page, save for a small note at the foot of it that read: 'This page has been deliberately left blank in accordance with the author's wishes.'

NOVEMBER 28

Before he was an injury-prone party animal, Lee Sharpe was an exciting young player with the world at his feet. Sir Alex Ferguson brought the winger to Manchester United from Torquay and today in 1990 he scored a hat-trick in a 6-2 rout of Arsenal at Highbury.

A less likely hat-trick hero is Paraguayan goalkeeper José Luis Félix Chilavert González who has an eye for goal, and not just in the last-second-of-the-game-might-as-well-go-up-for-a-corner type way. A free kick and penalty specialist, Chilavert scored more than 60 goals in his professional career and it was on this day in 1999 that he became the first (and as far as we can tell) only goalkeeper to score a hat-trick while playing for Argentine club Atlético Vélez Sársfield in their 6-1 win over Ferro Carril Oeste.

NOVEMBER 29

Today in 1899 one the biggest clubs in the world began what would become an illustrious history when FC Barcelona was founded. Despite being a fiercely Catalan institution, the club was founded by a Swiss named Joan Gamper who posted an advert in the newspaper calling for members for his new football club. It soon became an icon for the Catalan people, with the Camp Nou one of the only places they could express their regional identity without fear of reprisal under Franco's rule.

Also on this day in 1979 Viv Anderson became the first black player to represent England at senior level. Ron Greenwood selected the Nottingham Forest right-back for England's friendly match with Czechoslovakia at Wembley. England won the match 1-0 thanks to a Steve Coppell goal after a mistake by Czech keeper Pavol Michalik. Anderson went on to pick up 30 caps for his country.

NOVEMBER 30

On this day in 1991 the United States team beat Norway 2-1 to win the first ever women's World Cup in front of 65,000 fans in Guangshou's Tianhe Stadium, with USA striker Michelle Akers scoring a late winner for the Americans. In England, women had actually been banned from playing the game at Football League grounds in the 1920s when the FA decided it was not a ladylike pursuit. The ban was lifted in 1971 and since then the England women's team have eclipsed their male counterparts by winning a major trophy at the 2022 European Championship and reaching the World Cup final a year later.

On this day in 1991 the United States team beat Norway 2-1 to win the first ever women's World Cup in front of 65,000 fans in Guangshou's Tianhe Stadium, with USA striker Michelle Akers scoring a late winner for the Americans. In England, women had actually been banned from playing the game at Football League grounds in the 1920s when the FA decided it was not a ladylike pursuit. The ban was lifted in 1971 and since then the England women's team have largely mirrored their male counterparts: making it to the quarter-finals of two World Cups.

FOOTBALL
On This Day

DECEMBER

DECEMBER 1

Footballers lead a charmed life: a couple of hours training a day, match on a Saturday, fame and fortune, and the top players earn thousands of pounds a week. But even that isn't enough for some, as it was on this day in 2001 that a strike called by the PFA was due to start with Manchester United's clash with Chelsea the first high profile casualty. PFA chief Gordon Taylor was playing Arthur Scargill to Premier League boss Richard Scudamore's Maggie Thatcher, who declared it illegal before a compromise was eventually reached.

Darlington became the benefactors of Manchester United's decision to pull out of the FA Cup in 1999 as they were given a wildcard entry into the third round. Their fortune soon ran out though, as Aston Villa sent the Quakers packing with a 2-1 defeat as the Villains made it all the way to the final where they lost to Chelsea.

DECEMBER 2

Although the original Wembley Stadium had been closed for a couple of months, the English public were beginning to realise that their new national stadium might not be around as soon as they hoped, as a complete redesign was ordered today in 1999 when plans for an athletics track were scrapped. Little did they know, but the England team were embarking on eight years of hobo-like existence as a cast of characters including Ken Bates, the FA and a series of hapless government ministers brought the project home five years late and £500m over budget.

More bureaucratic goings-on today in 1902 as the Professional Footballers' Association was created at the Imperial Hotel in Manchester. Even back then money in football was an issue as Charlie Roberts and Billy Meredith set up the organisation in response to the Football League's creation of a £4 maximum wage a year earlier.

DECEMBER 3

In football it takes a brave man to jump ship to your most hated rivals. But then it also takes a brave man to sign Paulo Futre, so you can't accuse Harry Redknapp of never taking a risk. However, when Harry returned to Portsmouth today in 2005 after ditching Pompey for Southampton a year earlier, he was certainly stretching it. He would rub it in to Saints fans by saying: 'The last year has been the worst of my life and that is no exaggeration,' ensuring that he misses out on the red carpet treatment when he goes anywhere near St Mary's.

Too much wheeling and dealing had taken its toll on Wrexham today in 2004 as the Welsh side went into administration. The Robins were £2,600,000 in debt and were the first league club to suffer a ten-point deduction that saw them drop from mid-table to the foot of League One and subsequently condemned them to relegation.

DECEMBER 4

Is it true that referees never give penalties against Manchester United at Old Trafford? Well, today in 1993 Norwich's Ruel Fox scored from the spot and it was to be the last scored against United there for over 10 years, so we'll let you be the judge of that. Danny Murphy's winner from the spot in Liverpool's 1-0 win over United in April 2004 ended years of dodgy tackles, dives and refs bottling decisions under the duress of Roy Keane and pals.

United legend Bryan Robson was finding life in the dugout a smidgen harder than on the pitch, so today in 2000 the embattled Middlebrough manager was given the football equivalent of a pair of stabilisers as Terry Venables was brought in to steady the ship. Boro went on to beat the drop, finishing 14th, but Robbo didn't fancy flying solo at the end of the season so left to pave the way for Steve McClaren to take over.

DECEMBER 5

That old favourite Ebenezer Cobb Morley was in the news again today in 1863 as he carried on with his mission to turn football from a working class pastime into the all-conquering behemoth it is today, when he published the first set of rules in London newspaper *Bell's Life*. Ebenezer upset a few people as he banned picking up the ball and forbade 'tripping and hacking', but his 13 laws have remained largely untouched.

Newcastle United fans were probably wishing that Ebenezer hadn't bothered in 1908 as they suffered a humiliating 9-1 loss to Sunderland in a First Division match. Remarkably with half an hour left the Toon looked like they were going to get a result, but the Mackems went goal crazy, scoring eight times in the last 28 minutes in what remains their biggest and most satisfying league victory ever.

DECEMBER 6

If there's one thing you don't want to do in a Merseyside derby it's score an own goal. When the two rivals faced off today at Goodison in 1969 Everton defender Sandy Brown not only found the back of his own net, but did it in style. When a harmless-looking cross drifted into the Everton box, hard man Brown took it upon himself to deal with it, sprinting to the ball and planting a peach of a diving header into the back of the net to make him the toast of the wrong side of Merseyside.

Throughout his managerial career Brian Clough was plagued with accusations of illegal payments, with Terry Venables once claiming that 'Cloughie likes a bung'. It came as little surprise today in 1999 that the FA fined Nottingham Forest £25,000 for admitting unauthorised payments to managerial and playing staff between 1984 and 1993. Due to his failing health the FA never charged Ol' Big 'Ead himself.

LEEDS HARD MAN BILLY BREMNER IS ACCOSTED BY SPURS' DAVE MACKAY. BREMNER DIED IN DECEMBER 1997 (SEE OVER).

DECEMBER 7

Billy Bremner, the man who encapsulated Don Revie's great Leeds United side of the 60s and 70s, died today in 1997. Once described by *The Sunday Times* as '10 stone of barbed wire', Bremner joined Leeds as a 17-year-old after Arsenal and Chelsea turned him down for being too small. With a personal motto of 'side before self', Billy led Leeds throughout the most successful period in their history, proving you didn't have to be a six-foot bruiser to be the hard man.

Staying in Yorkshire, Scarborough's 1990 clash with Wrexham saw the lowest ever crowd for a Fourth Division match as only 625 showed their faces at Seamer Road in the pouring rain. The Seasiders won out 4-2 in a match where the programme was somewhat ominously sponsored by Black Death Vodka.

DECEMBER 8

It wasn't a bad time to be a German in 1991. The Berlin Wall was down, Maradona and the Argentines had been seen off in the World Cup final the previous year and today their captain Lothar Matthaus picked up the first ever FIFA World Player of the Year award. The point of the award isn't too clear, as the Ballon d'Or is still considered the most prestigious gong in world football, but we think the suits at FIFA fancied an excuse for another annual boozing session.

Player wages broke through the £50,000-a-week barrier today in 1999 when Roy Keane signed a new deal at Old Trafford. In return for playing the game he loves, Keano could now look forward to £52,000 appearing in his bank account once a week for the next four years. A goal in his next game against Valencia repaid the faith the Old Trafford money-men put in him.

DECEMBER 9

Ever wondered what Geordies got up to on Saturday afternoons before they could head over to St James' to whinge about their manager and show off their freshly tattooed bellies? No, neither have we, but all that began today in 1892 when Newcastle East End became Newcastle United and one of England's biggest clubs was born. Don't tell the Mackems, but until 1904 Newcastle sported some familiar sounding red and white stripes before the famous barcode shirts came into play.

In 2001 David Beckham became only the fourth footballer to win the BBC Sports Personality of the Year award. This was largely down to his heroics against Greece earlier in the year – including *that* injury time free kick – that secured England's place in the 2002 World Cup. Becks joined Bobby Moore, Paul Gascoigne and Michael Owen as the only footballers (at the time) to have picked up the award.

DECEMBER 10

Not a good day for Port Vale in 1892. Robbie Williams' favourite side went down 10-0 at home to Sheffield United in what still remains the record away win in Football League history.

There was to be no World Cup trophy-shaped Christmas present under the tree for the Three Lions, as another chapter in the book of heart-breaking major tournament exits was written. England headed to Qatar on the back of reaching the European Championship final just 18 months earlier, but a missed Harry Kane penalty with six minutes remaining of their quarter-final against France meant that a fine performance went unrewarded and the wait for silverware continued.

DECEMBER 11

Dial Square FC may sound like a random non-league side who should be playing the likes of Ebbsfleet United or Harrogate Railway, but they're far from it. It was today in 1886 that a Scotsman in north London called David Danskin got together with ten friends and colleagues to play the first game for a side that would eventually become Arsenal FC, after spells known as Royal Arsenal and then Woolwich Arsenal. Danskin and his mates got off to a flying start as they defeated Eastern Wanderers 6-0.

Staying in the capital, Queens Park Rangers broke their transfer record today in 1990 when they signed USA international Roy Wegerle from Luton Town for the princely sum of £1m. His first season at the club saw him finish third on the First Division's scoring table and win the Goal of the Season award for his mazy run and shot against Leeds United at Elland Road.

DECEMBER 12

In a blow to the image of hardened northerners everywhere, Blackburn Rovers fled the pitch against Burnley today in 1891 shortly after half-time as they were too cold. The two local rivals were playing out a bad-tempered match when all of the Blackburn side except for goalkeeper Herbie Arthur spat out the dummy and left the field of play. Play resumed with Arthur on his own and after he won a free kick for offside the game was abandoned as he had no one to pass to.

Further north Alex McLeish was turning up for his first day as Rangers manager in 2001, following Dick Advocaat's move upstairs to the position of general manager. During his four and a half years at Ibrox Big Eck won nine trophies, including the domestic treble in his first full season.

DECEMBER 13

Bryan Robson wasn't in the mood for messing around today in 1989 as the England captain scored the quickest ever goal in a professional match at the old Wembley Stadium when the Three Lions took on Yugoslavia. With just 38 seconds on the clock Captain Marvel fired home and put England on their way to 2-1 win and their 100th victory in the stadium.

Robbo's goalscoring feats paled in comparison next to the antics of French striker Stephane Stanis, today in 1942. Stanis' Racing Club side were pitted against Aubry-Asturies in the French Cup and he took no mercy on his opponents, bagging a world record 16 goals. Stanis' feat was equalled in 2007 when Olympos Xylofagou's wonderfully named striker Panagiotis Pontikos banged 16 against SEK Ayios Athanasios FC.

DECEMBER 14

Never has the result of a court case in Luxembourg meant so much to the game of football. Today in 1995 Jean-Marc Bosman won his landmark case in the European Court of Justice that forever changed the murky world of football transfers. Bosman had grown frustrated that he could not leave RFC Liege in 1990 when his contract expired, so took his club to court and a precedent was set granting players freedom of movement when their contracts had expired. The first team to be hit hard by the Bosman ruling were the reigning European Cup holders Ajax, who saw their young team ripped apart, losing the likes of Clarence Seedorf, Kanu, Patrick Kluivert and Edgar Davids.

Back in 1935 Ted Drake was doing his transfer value no harm when he bagged all seven goals for Arsenal in their 7-1 win over Aston Villa at Villa Park.

DECEMBER 15

After burning his bridges and slagging off most of his teammates in his infamous MUTV interview, Roy Keane joined Celtic on a free transfer today in 2005. Keano's spell at Celtic Park started disastrously as the Bhoys crashed out to Clyde in the Scottish Cup on Keane's debut, but the ship was steadied in time to win the title and League Cup before the Irishman retired at the end of the season.

A cardiac condition saw Sergio Aguero's career brought to a premature end today in 2021, just six months after he swapped Manchester City for Barcelona. Scorer of 184 Premier League goals for City, he provided perhaps the most iconic moment of the competition's history when he earned the Citizens their first top-flight title since 1968 with his late, late winner against QPR in 2012.

DECEMBER 16

Following his 11 game ban for pushing over referee Paul Alcock in 1998, Paolo Di Canio showed he wasn't all bad today in 2000 when he sportingly turned down a goalscoring opportunity for West Ham against Everton. With Everton keeper Paul Gerrard lying injured Di Canio chose to catch Trevor Sinclair's cross, rather than head the ball home and give the Londoners the lead in a close match. FIFA awarded the passionate Italian their Fair Play Award in 2001.

Back in Paolo's homeland in 1899 a group of bored British expatriates from Nottingham were forming one of the biggest clubs in the world. AC Milan started life as the Milan Cricket and Football Club, but when doubts were raised over whether the club could afford bats, football took over. According to founding member Herbert Kiplin, they styled their famous kit 'red to recall the devil, black to invoke fear.'

DECEMBER 17

Bobby Moore's growing reputation as one of the greatest defenders to ever play the game took a blow today in 1966 when his West Ham defence were put to the sword, conceding five goals to Chelsea. Luckily for Moore both sides were throwing caution to the wind in this London derby with the match ending up as a 5-5 draw.

Michael Owen capped off a fine year today in 2001 by picking up the prestigious Ballon d'Or award. Owen followed Liverpool's five trophies that year with a hat-trick in England's 5-1 win over Germany in Munich as he became the first English player to be named European Footballer of the Year since Kevin Keegan's perm won over hearts and minds in Germany whilst at Hamburg in 1979.

DECEMBER 18

Harry Redknapp's managerial career very nearly crashed and burned at the first hurdle today in 1982 when he took charge of his first match. After being appointed caretaker at Third Division Bournemouth, his team suffered a 9-0 defeat to high-flying Lincoln City. Asked if he was disappointed with the result, Redknapp merely said: 'Yes, I thought the seventh goal was offside.' But 'Arry soon got a grip, knocking holders Manchester United out of the FA Cup that very season.

The most controversial World Cup of modern times ended with the competition's greatest-ever final today in 2022. There were narratives a-plenty at the Lusail Stadium in Doha, in which a Lionel Messi vs Kylian Mbappé showdown lived up to the hype. Argentina were cruising at 2-0 with ten minutes left, only for an Mbappé brace to force extra time. Messi's second goal nudged his side ahead, only for Mbappé to complete his hat-trick to take the match to penalties. *La Albiceleste* would triumph and Messi had the World Cup win that affirmed his place in the pantheon of footballing immortals.

DECEMBER 19

Tony Adams hit rock bottom today in 1990 when he was sentenced to three months in prison for crashing his car whilst four times over the alcohol limit. Adams' well-documented drinking problem continued until he admitted he was an alcoholic in 1996 and sought help. He would later go on to set up the Sporting Chance clinic that helps professional sportsmen suffering from their various vices.

Also in the headlines for the wrong reasons was Rio Ferdinand in 2003 when he was banned for eight months after missing a drugs test. The FA took a hard-line stance on Ferdinand, not going in for Rio's defence that he was out shopping and forgot. The ban ruled Rio out of England's Euro 2004 efforts and made sure next time someone came a-calling with a little cup, Rio took notice.

DECEMBER 20

Middlesbrough manager Bryan Robson was left in a quandary today in 1996 when 23 of his players were either ill or injured ahead of their Premier League match against Blackburn. Robbo chose not to play the game, a decision that cost Boro big time as they were deducted three points by the league, which ultimately led to their relegation at the end of the season. In one of the unluckiest seasons ever seen, Boro also lost both the FA and League Cup finals.

Queens Park Rangers were the latest club to attract the rich and famous today in 2007 as steel magnate Lakshmi Mittal joined F1 tycoons Bernie Ecclestone and Flavio Briatore as investors at Loftus Road, making the Superhoops, somewhat surreally, the richest club in the world and making Roman Abramovich's roubles down the road look positively small time.

DECEMBER 21

Dutch conspiracy theorists were scratching their heads today in 1983 when their team missed out on a place at Euro 84 thanks to Spain's 12-1 win over Malta. The Spanish went into their final qualifier needing to win by 11 clear goals to make it to the finals and despite only leading 3-1 at half-time they managed it. Sceptical? Us? Never. The Maltese goalkeeper, John Bonello, has since gone down as a cult hero in Spain for his antics that night.

There was another daft scoreline in 1957 as Charlton trailed 5-1 to Huddersfield Town with half and hour remaining but somehow managed a 7-6 win. The Addicks had Johnny Summers to thank for their Lazarus-esque comeback as the left-winger bagged five goals to leave Town manager Bill Shankly shell shocked. The fightback was even more remarkable due to the fact that Charlton were playing with ten men when one of their players went down injured in those pre-substitute days.

DECEMBER 22

Deadly Doug Ellis got the chequebook out for once today in 2000 when he broke Aston Villa's transfer record by splashing out £9.5m on Colombian striker Juan Pablo Ángel. The former River Plate man's six years at Villa were hit and miss, seeing him bag 66 goals in 205 games for the club before he decided to take a punt on the MLS, joining New York Red Bulls and becoming the league's leading scorer in his first year.

Another former Villa striker was doing the business in 1990 as Gary Shaw turned out for Shrewsbury Town and bagged a hat-trick in 4 minutes and 32 seconds for the Salops. Shaw had been a part of Villa's 1982 European Cup winning side and had also picked up the Bravo Award, a trophy dished out by Italian magazine *Guerin Sportivo* for the best young player in Europe.

DECEMBER 23

It's the oldest trick in the book: getting sent off in your last match before Christmas so you don't have to worry about turning out on Boxing Day half-cut and full of turkey. In 1990 three players in the Leicester v Watford game were given their marching orders, taking the weekend's league total to 15, which was the worst in Football League history. *We know your game.*

In 2003 it looked like Darlington would also be having Christmas off as they were issued with a winding-up order. This was the culmination of chairman George Reynolds' chaotic five-year regime where the former safe-breaker and convict built a 26,000-capacity stadium that looked a tad pitiful with average crowds of 5,000, and loaded the club with debts before being thrown back in the slammer for tax evasion. The Supporters' Trust then stepped in to save the club from extinction.

DECEMBER 24

Liverpool manager Gérard Houllier indulged in a spot of Christmas shopping when he signed Czech Republic striker Milan Baroš from Baník Ostrava today in 2001. The 17-year-old cost Liverpool £3.3m, but the Euro 2004 top scorer never quite managed to match his international form at Anfield during his three years at the club.

Frank Swift, one of the forgotten victims of the Munich air disaster, was born today in 1913. The former England and Manchester City goalkeeper is regarded as one of the best English keepers of all time and became a journalist after he hung up his boots in 1949. Swift was part of the press pack that accompanied United on their ill-fated trip to take on Red Star Belgrade in 1958, and died on his way to hospital after being pulled alive from the wreckage.

DECEMBER 25

Never has the phrase 'football was the winner' been more apt than when the guns fell silent in the trenches of World War I in 1914 and British and German soldiers met in no-man's-land for a kick-about. After the Germans started singing carols, both sides put down their guns and met in the middle to exchange gifts and eventually a game of football broke out. The Germans are said to have won the match 3-2 (obviously), but for once it really was the taking part that counted.

Chelsea weren't getting into the spirit of giving today in 1948 when they launched the first ever programme at a football match, charging sixpence for the privilege. The 16-page programme for their Christmas Day clash with Portsmouth was a massive hit, with Arsenal the first to follow suit at the beginning of the next season.

DECEMBER 26

It's always fashionable to blame the influx of foreign players in the Premier League for the national side's shortcomings. Today in 1999 the anti-Johnny Foreigner bandwagon was in full effect as Chelsea became the first team to put out a side that didn't contain a single British player for their match with Southampton at the Dell. With players like Graeme Le Saux, Chris Sutton and Dennis Wise all missing, manager Gianluca Vialli opted for an all-foreign XI that managed to land Chelsea their first away win in three months as they beat Saints 2-1.

No such worries in 1935, as Tranmere showed you didn't need a star-filled team of internationals to know how to find the net. Rovers romped to a record 13-4 win over Oldham at Prenton Park. Robert 'Bunny' Bill was feeling particular rampant, scoring nine goals and missing a penalty to set a Football League record for most goals in a game.

DECEMBER 27

There were thieves at work on this day in 2005 when burglars broke into Anfield and stole the eight pennants that the club received during their victorious Champions League run earlier in the year. The Liverpool criminal underworld seem to have a grudge against Liverpool players, robbing the houses of Jerzy Dudek, Pepe Reina, Daniel Agger, Dirk Kuyt, Peter Crouch and Steven Gerrard during the Reds' Champions League away days, but before you point fingers at bitter Everton fans it's also worth remembering poor old Andy van der Meyde, whose dog was stolen, generating far more headlines than his owner ever did on the pitch.

Today in 1949 a record 1,269,934 were off to the football across the country, breaking the national attendance record. The average of 28,862 beat the record that was set just a day earlier as football was booming in post-war England.

DECEMBER 28

Whilst the catenaccio gripped 1960s Italian football and defences ruled supreme, here in Britain we were having none of it. Today in 1963, 66 goals were scored in the ten First Division matches played. Fulham were the day's top scorers, putting ten past Ipswich, while Blackburn beat West Ham 8-2 at the Boleyn Ground and West Brom played out a 4-4 draw with Spurs. We can only assume that the nation's defenders had gone overboard on turkey and had one too many shandies over their Christmas break.

That was also possibly Spurs' excuse in 1996 when Newcastle thrashed them 7-1 at St James' Park. Despite the deluge of goals all was not well in the Newcastle camp, as manager Kevin Keegan uncharacteristically refused to celebrate, and would resign two weeks later after becoming disillusioned with his board.

DECEMBER 29

Despite the season only being at the halfway stage Frank Clark became Manchester City's fifth manager of the campaign today in 1996. The Citizens were in a spot of bother following their relegation to the First Division the previous season and after a defeat to Barnsley that left them fourth bottom, caretaker Phil Neal did one, joining Steve Coppell, Asa Hartford and Alan Ball on the list of Maine Road flops that year.

Brazilian legend Pelé, considered by many to be the finest player the sport has ever produced, died today in 2022 at the age of 82. No player scored more than the 1,281 goals he netted during a 21-year career and he remains the only player to win the World Cup three times. A two-day public funeral in Brazil saw hundreds of thousands of fans flood the streets to pay their respects to football's first-ever global superstar.

DECEMBER 30

When Ian Wright was a struggling plasterer working for £100 a week before Crystal Palace took him on, he could not have imagined that he would end up receiving an honour from the Queen. But that's exactly what happened today in 1999 when the grinning goal machine from London was awarded an MBE by Her Majesty for services to football. Presumably those were services on the pitch and not in the commentary box.

When Brian Clough was awarded his (far more deserving) OBE he joked that it should stand for Ol' Big 'Ead. Today in 1989 he notched up his 1,000th game as manager when his Nottingham Forest side beat Tottenham 3-2 at White Hart Lane. Clough led Forest to their second consecutive League Cup that season, despite earning himself a lengthy touchline ban for clipping a pitch invader on the back of the head earlier in the year.

DECEMBER 31

Michael Owen ended the year on a downer in 2005, as he broke one of those pesky metatarsals after a collision with his England teammate Paul Robinson in Newcastle's 2-0 loss to Tottenham. After a race against time to be fit for the 2006 World Cup Owen barely made the squad, turning in two lacklustre performances before he snapped his anterior cruciate ligament against Sweden.

Whilst most people were out on the lash tonight in 1999, spare a thought for poor old Carlos Roa. The former Argentinian keeper and Seventh Day Evangelist retired from the game, gave away all his possessions and retreated to a mountain villa, where he expected the world to end as the new millennium was ushered in. Most famously known for being the keeper that Michael Owen had beaten to score his wonder goal in the 1998 World Cup, Roa declared that he needed to 'prepare for the end of the world, in a place where He will provide everything we need.'